From the Campfire to the HOLODECK

Creating Engaging and Powerful 21st Century Learning Environments

DAVID THORNBURG

Foreword by Prakash Nair

JB JOSSEY-BASS™

A Wiley Brand

Published by Jossey-Bass
A Wiley Brand
One Montgomery Street, Suite 1200, San Francisco, CA 94104-4594—www.josseybass.com

Jossey-Bass books and products are available through most bookstores. To contact
Jossey-Bass directly call our Customer Care Department within the U.S. at 800-956-7739,
outside the U.S. at 317-572-3986, or fax 317-572-4002.

Wiley also publishes its books in a variety of electronic formats and by print-on-demand.
Some material included with standard print versions of this book may not be included in
e-books or in print-on-demand. If the version of this book that you purchased references
media such as CD or DVD that was not included in your purchase, you may download this
material at http://booksupport.wiley.com. For more information about Wiley products, visit
www.wiley.com.

Library of Congress Cataloging-in-Publication Data
Library of Congress Cataloging-in-Publication Data has been applied for and is on file with
the Library of Congress.
ISBN: 9781118633939 (cloth); ISBN: 9781118633946 (ePub); ISBN: 9781118748060 (ePDF)

Printed in the United States of America

FIRST EDITION

HB Printing   V10010458_052319

Contents

[Schools] . . . have their indispensable office—to teach elements. But they can only highly serve us when they aim not to drill, but to create; when they gather from far every ray of various genius to their hospitable halls, and, by the concentrated fires, set the hearts of their youth on flame.

Ralph Waldo Emerson, 1837

Foreword

I still remember vividly my first encounter with David Thornburg's writings in early 2000 because of the profound impact it had on my work as a school architect. It is an influence that continues to affect our maturing practice at Fielding Nair International, where David's philosophies find creative expression every day throughout the United States and in many remote parts of the world.

My encounter with David's ideas came shortly after I had left my post as operations director for New York City's School Construction Program to start up my own consulting practice. During my stint with New York City, I had a key role in the creation of more than one hundred new schools and the modernization of at least five hundred old school buildings. My decision to leave my government job came shortly after my distressing realization that neither the new schools nor the "modernized" ones had done much to improve student educational achievement. On further examination, it became clear to me that we had spent about $10 billion on school buildings to reinforce what was, fundamentally, a flawed educational model. This model was all about the absorption and regurgitation of a static set of facts by students in a factory setting where the teacher firmly controlled both the inputs and outputs of education. Under this scheme, the rows and rows of identical classrooms along a double-loaded corridor sparsely furnished with cheap desks and chairs was the prevailing "design" of the day. Never mind that this identical design had been in place for nearly a century. That factor alone should have made us question if there was something wrong with our approach. However, to do so would have required us to question the nature of education itself, which would have led us to the rational conclusion that the predominant teacher-centered educational model of the day had gone past obsolescence and become, for the most part, irrelevant.

It is one thing to know that something needs to be done and another thing altogether to figure out exactly what to do or how to go about doing it. Education has been subjected to dozens of reform efforts since the 1980s, but, one could argue, very little seems to have actually changed in schools. Teachers continue to wield absolute control and students spend most of their school day on rote assignments. Much of their school day is spent preparing for tests by memorizing meaningless facts divorced from any real or deep understanding of the subject being studied. That said, there is still hope for our education system. Many effective reform efforts have taken root, and, although still small in scope and scale, the work by the tireless advocates for change is slowly beginning to bear fruit. One thing distinguishes this modern group of reformers from their predecessors. They are pragmatists, and their solutions are noted for their simple elegance and easy adoptability. Few reformers fit this description better than David Thornburg.

David came to prominence with his writings about the use of technology in schools and how this could be the game changer we had all been waiting for. Interestingly, when David first started writing about the subject, technology's promise to change education was still largely unrealized. In the 1980s and 1990s, governments had poured tens of billions of dollars into educational technology and had seen very little in the way of measurable returns. For example, I was personally aware of the way in which New York City wasted hundreds of millions of dollars with its policy to dump four computers in every middle school classroom. The problems with this approach are too numerous to list fully but consider that the city made no attempts to train teachers on how to use the technology, that large numbers of schools did not even have adequate outlets to plug in the new equipment, that schools had no internal network at that time for students to connect with each other and store their work, that there was no plan to connect the computers to the Internet, and there was no coherent plan to properly integrate technology into the curriculum.

This New York City example was, of course, an obviously broken technology program and not as big a concern for David because this dysfunction was evident to all. Instead, David had his eyes focused on schools and school districts that seemed to have their technology act together—where computer labs were humming smoothly and students were working with technology on a regular basis. In his earlier writings, and in this book as well, David asks us to look more closely at these schools. He instructs us—and I'm paraphrasing here—"Don't ask what you can do with computers but what can you do now that you have computers." Using this instruction as a guide, it became quickly apparent that most schools were asking the wrong question. They were asking, "What should we do with this technology?" Most of the time, they answered this question by using technology to simply reinforce the prevalent teacher-centered model. In this book, David points out the many ways in which technology continues to be used today to perpetuate teacher control and student dependence whether through rote technology-assisted assignments or by replacing older technologies such as the blackboard with newer technologies like SMART Boards without fundamentally changing the teacher-as-fountain-of-all-knowledge educational model.

In this book, David recounts briefly the story about how he came up with his "primordial learning metaphors." In a rapidly changing world whose only real guarantee is that nothing will stay the same for long, David asserts that in the education sphere there is actually some reassurance of constancy. Interestingly, this constancy relates to the way in which all of us, as human beings, learn. From primordial times, David says, humans have learned in four discrete ways—at the Campfire, at the Watering Hole, in the Cave, and from Life.

The Campfire mode of learning represents learning from a story-teller or an expert. In this form of learning, the learner is the passive recipient of information handed down from the teacher. Most modern schools, according to David, pervasively practice the Campfire form of learning in which a teacher, through lectures and other direct-instruction methods, controls what students learn and how they learn it.

If the Campfire represents learning from an expert, then the Watering Hole represents learning from one's peers. Watering Holes have the advantage in that, by their very nature, learning outcomes are unpredictable. No one knows exactly how a conversation with a peer or a group of peers will evolve, but it is a safe bet that the very nature of group interaction is such that they will elicit ideas beyond the narrow, defined scope of Campfire instruction. That said, Watering Hole learning may actually work better when it is stimulated by the storyteller at the Campfire. There is no question, however, that taken together the Campfire and the Watering Hole are better than either one of them on their own.

David then goes on to talk about Cave learning, which he describes as learning from oneself—through reflection and introspection. Citing Newton's aha moment when he "discovered" gravity during a time of quiet solitude interrupted by a falling apple, as well as his own discovery of a special kind of resistor to measure electric current (now used worldwide in Duracell batteries), David shows how creativity is encouraged by Cave learning.

The fourth primordial learning metaphor is Life. This is when the other forms of learning get an opportunity for a trial run. It represents all forms of applied learning when theory is put into practice. Life is necessary to close the loop on learning in the same way that learning about driving a car from an expert, talking about it with a friend, and then reflecting on it by oneself will only go so far. Only when one gets behind the wheel of the car does the real purpose of the other forms of learning become apparent and real.

David goes on to talk about the importance of space and place as well as the appropriate technologies necessary to fully realize their value in school. He asks educators to balance student educational experiences so that they spend the appropriate amount of time in each of the four forms of learning and to reduce their reliance on the Campfire form of learning. Naturally, this will require some rethinking about school design—something that we, in our practice, have been forced to do as a consequence of providing students with equal access to all four forms of learning. Schools designed or modernized from the ground up using David Thornburg's primordial learning metaphors, upgraded to reflect today's technological world, will look very different from their industrial age counterparts. (You will find many such examples of new paradigm schools at http://designshare .com and http://fieldingnair.com.)

David asks educators to stay focused on the ultimate purpose of education in a world where data and information are readily available at the touch of a button. Today, more than ever before, we need to educate our children so they "not just learn about events but the meaning behind the events."

In his concluding chapter, David demonstrates a method that all schools can benefit from to bring the learning contained in the book to fruition. This is his design of the Educational Holodeck, a simulated environment in which students' rich learning experiences are limited only by their own imagination. In the holodeck, students go beyond the memorization of static facts toward gaining real, lasting, and meaningful knowledge based on a deep understanding of the subject being studied. It is easy to see how the holodeck can provide the holistic learning experience in which students move easily and seamlessly among all four primordial learning metaphors of Campfire, Watering Hole, Cave, and Life. In doing so, they use the mode of learning that best suits the challenges at hand in solving the complex problems contained within each holodeck adventure.

In the end that may be the best message this book sends—that real learning is an adventure, like life itself. Only by recognizing this simple truth can our schools go beyond rote learning to a model that is as engaging as it is rigorous in learning environments that are also designed to reflect this new model.

Prakash Nair
President, Fielding Nair International

About the Author

Since the early 1980s, David Thornburg, PhD, has authored numerous books and hundreds of articles on the uses of emerging technologies in education. He is a frequent presenter at major educational technology conferences and a part-time faculty member of Walden University. His interest in topics related to this book comes from the realization that technologies can be used to do old things differently or to do new things that were not possible before. It is this latter use that keeps him active in the field, working with schools, districts, and governments to transform education for the benefit of students and teachers alike.

Prior to embarking on his career in education, David spent the 1970s at the Xerox Palo Alto Research Center (PARC), where, among other things, he invented some user-interface tools for computers still in use today. Because of his deep personal understanding of technology, he has the ability to look beyond the boxes and focus on how they are used. This is reflected in his work as well as in the book you are about to read.

Acknowledgments

Unlike Athena, books like this do not spring fully formed from the head of Zeus. As you will see, the ideas in this book evolved over decades. Much early help came from Prasad Kaipa. Later, I benefited from conversations with Prakash Nair, who graciously consented to write the foreword to this book.

My wife, Norma, has been amazingly supportive of me, especially when I entered "book writing mode," an altered state of consciousness that stays active even as I'm attempting to do other things. Kate Bradford at Jossey-Bass improved this text through careful editing. Her work helped me express the underlying ideas in this book with greater clarity, and she has my deepest thanks for this effort.

Introduction

In 1996 I published the book *Campfires in Cyberspace*.[1] In the introduction, I said, "This is yet another book about educational technology—a topic that has been hotly debated for many years, and is likely to be talked about for many more to come."

As I reflect today on that opening sentence, I am astounded at how wrong I was. This was *not* a book about technology. It may have been a book about media—of which modern computers, the Internet, and powerful applications are a part—but it was primarily a book about how humans develop an understanding of topics of interest to them: academic subjects in school, work-related ideas in business, basically the development of understanding in any domain. Although computers, smartphones, tablets, and other modern gadgets have roles to play in this quest, so do the physical spaces in which understanding is developed. Whether talking about the classroom or office workplace, the layout of physical environments and the tools used there matter.

In that earlier book, the focus on media was reflected through thoughts I first learned from Marshall McLuhan—a man whose ideas infested and warped (for the better, I think) the thinking of many people. His perceptions remain as relevant today as they ever were, and this book continues to look at the world partly through lenses he helped craft.

The years since 1996 have seen tremendous changes in technologies and have provided me with the time to reflect on the underlying ideas behind that book to the point that I realized it was time to revisit the topic from a new perspective. It is not that the insights I presented were wrong; it is that I did not realize at the time the extent of the power hidden in them. And this has caused me to write a new book on the topic. This book is not a rehash of old ideas but is an elaboration on the core concepts informed by many years of personal experience and through rich conversations with others.

The original ideas that triggered *Campfires in Cyberspace* grew out of a conference I attended at the National Academy of Sciences in the early 1990s. When I received the invitation a few weeks before, I knew it was an event I could not miss. The speakers were diverse in their backgrounds and professions but were all what I called *picture cards*, people who had risen to leadership positions in their fields because of their capacity to see beyond the present and to craft powerful and articulate visions of the future. In fact, had any one of the presenters been giving a speech, I would have attended. Senators and science fiction authors shared the podium with other politicians and pundits. And so it was that five hundred or so of us were jammed into the auditorium at the National Academy to take part in one of the finest gatherings of diverse experts ever assembled. Arthur C. Clarke presented (by video conference) from Sri Lanka. Other science fiction authors (Bruce Sterling, William Gibson) gave presentations about the future of learning through their respective lenses in person. Other presenters ranged from the very young (a school child) to the more seasoned (a senator or two). And, if the presenters were amazing, so was the audience. Corporate executives, world-class educators, staff from the White House, Departments of Labor, Education, and Commerce were all in attendance. This was to be a very intense learning experience.

Which is why what happened next is so interesting.

After about two hours of nonstop presentations, some in the audience left the room to use the restrooms. Interestingly, on their return, many stayed in the hall talking with others about what they had just been hearing. It was as if conversation with colleagues was more important at that moment that hearing from more world leaders in the field of technology and its possible impact on learning. The presentations were being given one after the other, with no scheduled breaks until lunch. For some people, this was just too much information to assimilate without talking about it with others.

The first night, I just needed to reflect on the events of the day by myself, putting everything into context and thinking about next steps. On my flight home, I came to the realization that I had just seen evidence of three learning spaces: Campfires (home of the lecture), Watering Holes (home to conversations with peers), and Caves (places of quiet reflection). Soon after I returned, I had lunch with a good friend, Prasad Kaipa. During this lunch I outlined my ideas about Campfires, Watering Holes, and Caves. He pointed out that I was missing one more space—that of Life—the domain where what we've learned gets applied.

Could it be that humans have always occupied these diverse learning spaces, moving between them as needed? Do these spaces apply to learning in other cultures? What role can technology play in support of these spaces? How does the physical layout of a learning environment affect the kinds of learning that takes place there? These were all questions that floated in my mind as I continued to write, give speeches, and conduct workshops on the topic.

In retrospect, I could have had these ideas earlier. In the 1970s while I was working at the Xerox Palo Alto Research Center (PARC), my research on the development of computer user interfaces took place in several environments. Attending formal presentations was one venue through which my mind was stimulated—benefiting from the Campfire. But another important part of my work involved conversations and collaborations with my peers—spending time at the Watering Hole. And, when working on a particularly challenging problem, I would lock myself in my office or go to a quiet spot off campus to think through ways of addressing the challenge. These places became my Cave. Finally, when I built a prototype and tried it out, I was occupying the space of Life.

Of course, in the beginning, my use of "spaces" was largely metaphorical—we each occupy different spaces from time to time in our quest as learners, even if these spaces are mental constructs. In other words, the idea of four learning spaces is a bigger concept than we might think. However, on further reflection, I observed that traditional schools tended to be very Campfire focused, and it was natural to look for connections between the learning space (the Campfire) and the physical space (the classroom) where this model of learning was dominant.

I was delighted to find out, years later, that some of my ideas were helping architects think through new designs for schools—especially through the work of the firm Fielding Nair, whose partners even wrote a book, *The Language of School Design*, on the topic.[2] Prakash Nair, a partner in the firm, says that traditional schools are driven by "cells and bells." The cells represent the fixed classrooms and the bells signal when it is time for students to move from one cell to another. His designs are a refreshing break from this model!

Some of these questions became the topic of my first book. Other questions emerged since that book was written. Much of my work in the intervening years ended up being shaped by these ideas—and this book you are holding reflects my current thinking on the topic.

It should be noted that the ideas presented here apply in lots of places—workplaces as well as schools. They apply to both formal and informal learning. And the journey is far from over.

CHAPTER 1

The Problem with Traditional Classrooms

Place matters in education—it always has, and it always will.

Of all the places I remember from my childhood, school was one of the most depressing. My school was a rectangular box filled with identical rooms, each of which had the same uncomfortable furniture bolted to the floor. The walls were drab and the front of the room was dominated by a large blackboard before which my teachers presided. The windows in the room typically looked out onto the street where, at least, one might glimpse cars passing by. However, looking out the window was frowned on because it showed disrespect for the teacher—and anything that violated the "eyes-front" rule resulted in a trip to the principal's office—where, at least, the waiting room chairs were more comfortable.

In later years, at other schools, I was treated to chairs with built-in "desks" on the right side of the seat. Because I was left-handed, this configuration was painful to endure because I had no place to rest my arm as I was writing. One teacher even went so far as to ask that I learn to write with my right hand—to modify myself to match the furniture. As a result, I am now ambidextrously dysgraphic.

Yes, this depiction sounds severe, and perhaps I have chosen only to emphasize the bad parts—but the fact that bad parts even existed

1

makes my point even more strongly. Childhood should be a time of joyous exploration—of play and discovery. Yes, there exists a real need for the didactic presentation of information; and the acquisition of skills, no matter how important they might be, can sometimes look very repetitive and mind-numbing.

It wasn't until decades later—long after my schooling was a distant memory—that I started wondering why my elementary and middle schools looked the way they did.

When I started speaking at educational conferences, I glibly argued that the reason for poor design was that schools, prisons, and mental hospitals were the only three places in society where, if you didn't go, someone came and got you. If attendance wasn't voluntary, why make it inviting?

But I was wrong, very wrong. The challenge of school design has been with us for ages—in fact ever since formal schools were created. This is reflected in the amazing painting of a classroom at the University of Bologna by Laurentius de Voltolina created around 1350 (see figure 1.1).

This all-too-recognizable picture of a classroom shows a teacher at the front, lecturing to a room full of students, only a few of whom are paying attention. Some are sleeping, others are talking, and some are probably just letting their minds wander. How effective could this model of education be? In all likelihood, it was not very effective then, nor has it been in the centuries that have passed since this picture was painted. Yes, perhaps some students did well in this environment, but many others did not.

And (as we'll explore soon), the problem is not necessarily the teacher but the environment in which the teacher is forced to work. Physical environments that impede learning hurt teachers as well as students. Some have said it isn't *dyslexia* but *dysteachia*, but, in fact, it may be *dysfacilitia*. The time is long overdue to shift the blame for a failed system from the teachers to the facilities themselves.

The idea that facilities shape educational practice is not new. In 1928, Harold Rugg and Ann Shumaker wrote *The Child-Centered*

Figure 1.1
Source: Classroom picture painted by Laurentius de Voltolina, c. 1350, from http://en.wikipedia.org/wiki/File:Laurentius_de_Voltolina_001.jpg.

School: An Appraisal of the New Education, a book about the rise of progressive education started by John Dewey and his contemporaries in response to the then-popular factory model of schooling found throughout the country. As the authors wrote,

> Not long ago news reels were flashing on the screen scenes of the desolation left in the wake of a cyclone which had swept the Middle West. The camera played over homes and villages which had been splintered into matchwood, and suddenly, amid the debris, the remains of a schoolhouse appeared. Walls and roof had been ripped off, but there still tightly screwed to the uptilted floor, stood rows of rigid schoolroom desks and chairs Untouched,

Immovable, more Inexorable than Fate itself they stood—mute symbols of an unyielding discipline!

Desks in rows! A characteristic setting for the traditional education, and typical of its spirit, too. Desks in rows to prison unwilling and recalcitrant youth while education laid its heavy yoke upon them. Children required to sit still—freedom of movement denied them. Repressed and quiet, they were crowded into huge classes where personal identities were thwarted if not entirely submerged.

Here order and quiet were the prerequisites of the educative process. Having chained the pupil to his desk and by a rigorous discipline subdued all overt physical activity, the old school proceeded to teach him.

For it was with the minds of pupils that the older education was chiefly concerned. Pupils sat at their desks all day, studying and reciting. The curriculum was crowded with subjects through which the pupils passed to the accompaniment of a continual dread of examinations marks, reports. What need had this educational regime for other than the stock materials—books of texts, blackboards, papers, pencils, a map or two?[1]

Rugg wrote from the perspective that schools were about to change for the better—to leave outmoded models behind. His goal, like that of most progressive educators, was to make learning an adventure, not a dreaded chore. History has (unfortunately) proved him wrong. Schools did not abandon the failed practices of the past. If anything, they have been reinforced and even perpetuated through the inclusion of new technologies that do nothing to address the core issue. Take, for example, the rapid growth of interactive whiteboard installations in schools. These expensive devices perpetuate the model of education that has the teacher at the front of the room with the students (primarily) listening to a presentation—the very model known to have been a failure since 1350!

More recently, this topic was revisited in a series of articles in *New Directions for Teaching and Learning* describing how furniture selection and layout affected college education.[2] Several articles in that journal show the connection between classroom layout and constructivist education, a connection that will be explored later in this book. Another book on the topic by Richard Gerver addresses the challenge and bemoans the fact that most modern schools have all but destroyed the creative impulses of children.[3] He asks a bold question: "Why can't schools be as exciting as Disney World?"

But one does not need scholarly journals and books to find the problem—one need only ask the teachers themselves. In some of our workshops, teachers are asked to design their ideal classroom. Rarely, if ever, do these designs bear any resemblance to the traditional classrooms of our youth. For example, a reading resource teacher submitted the following concept: she wanted a special room for reading with a tumbling mat in the center with nice cushions for those children who like to read lying down. To the left were hanging egg chairs for those kids who like to be cocooned while reading. The rest of the room had tables, computers, bookcases, and a fireplace (this teacher works in an area that gets quite cold in the winter). She also wanted a loft for herself where she could work one-on-one with a child without drawing undue attention from the rest of the class. In her dream classroom, she neither had, nor wanted, a desk of her own on the main floor.

GETTING TO A STATE OF FLOW

So far, we've presented the case that traditional classrooms are failing to meet the learning needs of many students and that the redesign of facilities can play an important role in rectifying this situation. But what deeper basis drives the suggestion that place matters so much?

An answer can be found through the application of the theory of flow developed decades ago by Mihalyi Csikszentmihalyi.[4] In an excellent series of books, he describes the characteristics of intrinsic

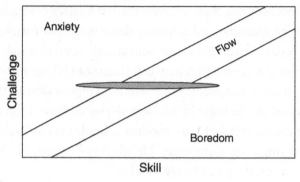

Figure 1.2

motivation and the importance of a state of being he calls *flow*. Basically, he makes the observation that we face challenges with a set of skills. Our reaction to the challenge depends on our skill level as shown in figure 1.2.

In this figure we can see what happens in different situations involving challenge and skill. If the challenge greatly exceeds the student's skill, anxiety sets in. When the skill of the learner is much higher than the challenge, the student is bored. But when skill and challenge are matched, we enter a region called *flow*—a space that is home to optimal experiences.

We've all experienced flow—perhaps when engrossed in a great book, an engaging athletic activity, or challenging (and rewarding) work. Students can (and should) experience flow in the classroom as well as outside of school. When school induces flow states, students want to stay after the end of the day—they show up early and are eager to take part in their activities. But consider what happens when we emphasize lectures in the classroom. In this case, the challenge is fixed by the teacher (represented by the gray, elongated oval in the figure). Faced with this static challenge, some students may bring low levels of skill and become anxious. Still others may have much higher levels of skill and become bored. Those for whom challenge and skill are matched have the potential to experience flow, and for these students traditional schooling may work pretty well.

But, the traditional school doesn't work for everyone, or even most students, suggesting that a heavily lecture-based pedagogy is flawed if our goal is to reach every learner. Look at the painting by de Voltolina again to see the consequences of this approach. Of course, there is more recent evidence of the problem. Csikszentmihalyi and his colleagues have conducted studies in which students respond to beepers during various activities and report on their levels of engagement while listening to adults talk.[5] For example, in an honors history class in which the teacher was lecturing about Genghis Khan's invasion of China, students used beepers that, when triggered, told them it was time to report on their levels of engagement. Of twenty-seven students in the class, only two were thinking about China; and of those two, one was thinking about Chinese food and the other was wondering if Chinese men wear their hair in ponytails. Although there is no one single pedagogical approach suited for all students, there is one approach that goes a long way toward addressing the challenge of getting all students to enjoy a state of flow: inquiry-driven, project-based learning.

The development of inquiry-driven, project-based learning, like many of the other innovations described in this chapter, is not new. Similar to many innovations, it was the development of thinkers in the field of progressive education. William Kilpatrick at Columbia University wrote an article on the "project method" many years ago. In this article he made the following point regarding projects as "purposeful acts":

How then does the purposeful act utilize the laws of learning? A boy is intent upon making a kite that will fly. So far he has not succeeded. The purpose is clear. This purpose is but the "set" consciously and volitionally bent on its end. As set the purpose is the inner urge that carries the boy on in the face of hindrance and difficulty. It brings "readiness" to pertinent inner resources of knowledge and thought. Eye and hand are made alert. The purpose acting as aim guides the boy's thinking, directs his examination of

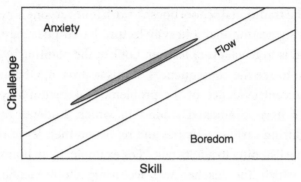

Figure 1.3

plan and material, elicits from within appropriate suggestions, and tests these several suggestions by their pertinency to the end in view. The purpose in that it contemplates a specific end defines success: the kite must fly or he has failed. The progressive attaining of success with reference to subordinate aims brings satisfaction at the successive stages of completion . . . The purpose thus supplies the motive power, makes available inner resources, guides the process to its pre-conceived end and by this satisfactory success fixes in the boy's mind the successful steps as part and parcel of one whole. The purposeful act does utilize the laws of learning.[6]

If students are engaged in acts they consider to be purposeful, what happens to our challenge and skill diagram? The oval representing the distribution of the challenge to students in the classroom shifts as shown in figure 1.3.

This figure suggests that, when students are allowed to work at projects based on their own skill levels, they create challenges that move them into the optimal area where challenge and skill are balanced. But given that a goal of education is skill development, how does this realignment help?

Basically, as students work on their projects, they increase their skills to the point that they enter the flow state. How does this happen? If they maintain the same challenge, they begin to become bored, so they increase their own challenge. The result is a staircase of skill development taking place near the flow boundary, with each student moving at his or her own pace. And, if students are in flow, then most likely the teachers are as well.

With all the power of project-based learning, it is logical to ask why this pedagogical model has not become commonplace. One argument is that the US focus in education has been driven during the first decade of this century by high-stakes testing that caused educators to focus on helping students score well on those tests. This test-driven approach to education was seen to be dependent on lectures and readings. The idea of students doing projects on their own, in which the curricular outcomes of these projects could not be determined in advance, was seen as cutting into the school day rather than enhancing it. In many cases, the effect of these laws stripped creativity and innovative problem solving from the curriculum. But, with the rise of new standards (for example, the Next Generation Science Standards (www.nextgenscience.org/next-generation-science-standards), this situation will change in fundamental ways. First, rather than focusing purely on content, the new standards address thinking strategies and the transferability of ideas across disciplines. These standards open the door for the widespread adoption of inquiry-driven, project-based learning.

The adoption of new standards is not enough. Fundamental changes in teaching strategies take a long time to adopt. Our own experience in this area suggests that up to three years of ongoing staff development are needed to be sure the changes have really taken hold. Some strategies for helping the migration to project-based learning will be explored later in our technology section.

Engagement is the key objective. With the goal of creating environments that engage challenged learners and provide opportunities for flow, we now start our exploration of the four primordial learning spaces mentioned in the introduction to this book—the Campfire, Watering Hole, Cave, and Life. Each of these has a role to play in the crafting of educational activities that engage students at any age and in any subject.

CHAPTER 2

Campfires

From chapter 1, it might seem that I'm arguing that lectures have no place in education. That, in fact, is not true. Yes, we have a system that seems overly reliant on teacher presentations, but from the beginning, education probably started with apprenticeship and storytelling. Apprenticeship provided the practical skills (hunting, cooking, fabric making, etc.) and storytelling provided the deeper understanding of the mysteries of life itself. One challenge may be that, over millennia, the role of apprenticeship has declined and that of storytelling has increased to the point that many schools no longer offer lab courses or other opportunities for children to build things, relying instead on a combination of teacher presentations and assigned readings from textbooks. Exceptions to this exist, of course, but the old model is still in place in too many schools.

As this chapter's title indicates, our subject is the Campfire—one of four learning spaces that stretches back to the beginnings of humanity. The Campfire is, for many cultures, home to storytelling—a place where people gather to hear stories told by others. Many of these stories evolved into myths that were used to explain the complexities of existence. One (of many) incredibly rich examples of this kind of story can be found in the legends of the Northwest Indian cultures in North America. Many stories in this tradition involved the escapades of Raven—a trickster—whose adventures explained the origin of day and night cycles and many other things. One fine example of this kind of story can be found in Raven stories told by Pacific Northwest

Indians.[1] These stories were the primary method that knowledge of the universe was shared with youngsters. The use of primordial archetypes (trickster, etc.) made them particularly engaging. This engagement was essential in preliterate societies because oral tradition was the only way to pass stories from one generation to another and it was important that the stories be remembered.

Because the storytellers were the keepers of knowledge in preliterate times, they wielded enormous power—a power that has remained in the hands of teachers today, even in a textbook-driven educational system. Of course, today, the Campfire has been replaced by the interactive whiteboard in many classrooms, but the underlying pedagogical implication remains the same as it was at the dawn of history: teachers are the arbiters of knowledge. The challenge is for teachers to know not just when to provide presentations to students and when to let them learn through other activities, but also what and how much to present. Although the teacher's position as knowledge deliverer can definitely be taken to extremes, there are still times when students need to be "told" something—and for this the lecture is appropriate.

If we think of the lecture as storytelling, one question we need to ask is just how much of the story should be told? For example, students need to be told about the properties of numbers and even have the concepts demonstrated to them. But math teachers know that student skills in this area transcend memorization. It is through student demonstrations that math skills are developed and refined. The alternative is often not pretty to see.

Many years ago I was consulting for the State of California on a new mathematics initiative in which students were presented with problems about which questions could be asked. One such problem involved a triangle as shown in figure 2.1. The question was whether this triangle could be constructed and what reasoning led to the conclusion.

One student (correctly) said that the triangle could not be constructed. His reasoning, however, was quite flawed. He wrote that the triangle could not be built because $40^2 + 60^2$ did not equal 90^2.

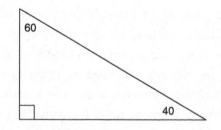

Figure 2.1

In other words, on seeing what appeared to be a right triangle, the student had tried to use the Pythagorean theorem, which he had memorized but applied incorrectly. Because the length of the sides was not specified, the student blindly replaced side length with angles, assuming that this would work equally well. This is the kind of response that results from rote learning.

As long as teaching is dominated by the presentation of material (including that in textbook form), we risk perpetuating wrong approaches to open-ended challenges. Mathematics is not alone—I remember having a world history teacher who convinced us that history was nothing but lists of names, dates, battles, and places. He never explored the story behind the story. As a result, I had an active dislike for the subject until I took a US history course taught by a gifted man whose PhD thesis was about the conditions leading to the construction of the Panama Canal. This may sound to you like one of those deadly dull topics that would make high school students fall asleep immediately. His classes contained some presentation of material, of course, but this was peppered with various back stories lending intrigue to the topic, and plenty of opportunity to explore what-if scenarios. As a result, I completely changed my views of history as a topic of study. It was exciting! It was relevant! I could even (at the time) see myself someday becoming an historian.

My teacher didn't teach me history; he taught me to think like a historian—and these are two different things. Both of these approaches can be addressed in the classroom Campfire setting. As the old song says, "T'aint what you do, it's the way that you do it."

Opportunities abound to magnify the power of lectures many times over. The challenge is to present just enough information to set the stage for student discovery, and then to set students free to find the material they need themselves. Lectures still have a huge role to play in education. However, lectures in a school setting can be improved by framing them as tools for providing the context for student research, with the content coming (largely) from the students themselves.

For example, instead of giving a lecture on the Moors in the Iberian Peninsula, the teacher might start by showing pictures of Portuguese churches built during that time and ask students why these churches also looked like forts. At this point, students could gather in groups and conduct their own research and prepare a presentation to the rest of the class. This kind of activity is likely to bring students in contact with far richer and more voluminous material on the subject than is covered in any textbook or lecture on the topic. The lecture's role in this case is to set the stage for student projects—a well-known and highly effective method of teaching reaching back to the progressive ideas of Dewey and his colleagues.

The formulation of project starters—brief presentations that set up a driving question—is something my wife, Norma, and I have been doing for years. We like to create short (typically one-minute) videos that give just enough background information to set the stage for the question. The students respond to the question by doing research and creating a project to reflect their discoveries. I will explore the technology behind these project starters in a later chapter on technology. For now, just know that by using a short video clip, the teacher is able to resist the temptation to blurt out the answers. (For sample project ideas and videos, go to http://knights-of -knowledge.com/projects.html.)

The tendency to give too much information is driven by our pride in our own knowledge and our desire to share that knowledge with our students. The problem is that by doing that, we destroy the chance for students to make discoveries on their own, and perhaps even learn new things of which the teacher is unaware.

I had an interesting example of this when a science teacher asked me to take his class on a tour of the solar system using special software I was using in another project. After looking at the eight planets, one student asked, "Why is it the inner four planets are rocky and the outer four are gaseous?" At this point the teacher got up to give the answer and I signaled for him to sit down. I told the student that this was an interesting question that she could research and present a report on her findings the following week. The teacher saw what I did and liked it. Whether this approach has permeated his teaching I don't know, but I was happy to model the kind of pedagogy that led to interesting questions.

Teachers, in designing their Campfire experiences for kids, might adopt the view of the French mathematician and philosopher, Henri Poincaré, who is reported to have said, "The question is not 'What is the answer?' The question is 'What is the question?'" To me this is an important distinction for the following reason. When we give students answers to questions, their learning stops—our content has placed a ceiling on their future learning of the topic. But when we formulate engaging questions and then allow students to explore them in their own projects, we have given them a floor on which future learning can take place in an area, perhaps for a lifetime.

The challenge is that good questions are tricky to formulate. The most interesting ones are called *driving questions* and they lead to student projects that can trigger deep exploration in a content area. In our workshops we have teachers write questions they think are interesting and then look at them to see if they can be written in a way that leads to deeper exploration. For example, a teacher might ask, "How can you cut a pizza so it can be shared equally by two people?" Contrast that with the question, "Given that the first cut does not go through the center of the pizza, how can a pizza be cut so it can be shared equally by two people?" Next, ask, "What happens if you have a third person join you and you want to be sure everyone gets exactly the same amount of pizza?" The first question might be used to explore the idea of fractions. The next question goes deeper into the mathematics of topology and can trigger some great explorations by students of nearly any age.

CHAPTER 3

Watering Holes

If the Campfire is home to the didactic presentation of material, the Watering Hole is the place for social learning among peers. This learning takes place through conversations, not lectures. Each of us takes part in the Watering Hole—whether it is the water cooler or copying machine at work, the lunchroom, or any other gathering place where peers interact—social learning is a dominant activity in all societies and always has been. In a recent interview with Brazilian communication expert Clóvis De Barros Filho in the Revista TAM magazine, *Nas Nuvens*, he described dialogue this way:

Dialogue is precisely that moment in which people say things they would not say if they weren't conversing with another person. It's the opportunity to produce knowledge and a way of thinking that's different from when people are alone. They are stimuli that redirect thought with each intervention. This means that the outcome of the dialogue is absolutely unexpected and virginal in relation to the original repertoires of the people speaking. Individual A, with all his or her repertoire, meets individual B. Well, the dialogue is not A + B in any way. Nor is it the combination of A with B or an intersection of A with B. It's something else. People involved in a dialogue end up saying things they hadn't planned to say, but needed to say because of an intervention from the outside world.[1]

This quality of dialogue—a characteristic of the Watering Hole—is tremendously important in the domain of education. Lev Vygotsky, the father of social constructivism, makes reference to the *zone of proximal development*—the domain where a learner may be ready to advance to the next step of understanding but is triggered to this new level by the social interaction of a teacher or a peer.[2]

As for where this triggering may take place, it doesn't much matter. It can be inside or outside the school. The critical element is that it takes place in a social environment in which conversation is not only permitted, but it is also encouraged.

In the late 1970s and early 1980s, I taught graduate courses part-time at Stanford University. I always had the last periods of the day and this was wonderful because, after class, some of us would head down the street into Palo Alto where we would convene at a local bookstore-coffee shop. Our conversations were generally quite rich and sometimes went into the late evening hours. What I especially liked about the informality of this environment is that I was learning as much as the students—we were truly co-learners long before the term became popular. Perhaps it was experiences like this that caused Marshall McLuhan to suggest that education might be improved if the universities shut down and the students and faculty just met in pubs.

This is a severe extrapolation. As mentioned previously, lectures do have their place, but the learning opportunities afforded by dialogue are profoundly important and are too infrequent when students are seated in rows facing the front of the room.

When I worked at the Xerox Palo Alto Research Center, the architect Gyo Obata designed our new building to encourage spontaneous meetings in the hallways. In fact, comfortable couches and dry marker boards were scattered throughout the building and outside the offices to facilitate just the kind of Watering Hole experiences described in this chapter. For larger groups, we even had some rooms that were mostly empty except for some beanbag chairs in which people would sit to have conversations (see figure 3.1). At least one wall of these rooms was a dry marker surface to facilitate group brainstorming.

Figure 3.1

And this is not all we had. In addition to comfortable seating that encouraged conversation, we had a wonderful cafeteria and another room with both pool and table tennis tables. The idea of a bunch of scientists locked away in their labs and offices was foreign to those of us who worked there. Of course, we had offices and even an auditorium where we would hear presentations from time to time, but the care taken in the design of conversational spaces had a lasting impact on many of us.

As for the success of this approach, the computer on which this book was written has a graphical user interface, a mouse, an Ethernet connection, and connection to a laser printer—all of which were invented or (in the case of the mouse, refined) at Xerox PARC in the 1970s. Although I can't speak for others, my own experience was that the Watering Hole environments there made it easy for me and others to engage in crossdisciplinary projects, many of which emerged serendipitously. For example, although I had my own research responsibilities in the area of device physics, I also would hang out with the systems scientists one floor up, where, among other things, I was able to invent the resistive touch tablet still in wide use today. These kinds of inventions were born from chance encounters with people across disciplines who shared their needs and others who had skills no one had thought about before.

Google and other companies champion this approach. Google even has some multi-rider conference bicycles that allow up to seven people to sit in a circle and talk while they are headed to another building together for a meeting.

Of course, one of the challenges of the Watering Hole is scale. Unlike lectures that can be delivered to hundreds or more at the same time, real conversations typically involve four or fewer people. In fact, theoretical models (coupled with observations) show that, over time, conversational groups devolve to two or three members no matter what their size when starting out.[3] Larger conversational groups may start off with one conversation taking place, but over time people drop out of the larger group and re-form smaller groups. This process continues until there are multiple groups of only two or three participants, each group being involved with its own conversation.

With this characteristic of group dynamics in place, it is little wonder that formal schools have so little opportunity in their buildings for Watering Hole events. Instead of fostering this important mode of learning, students may gather in the lunchroom, playground, or locker area. One reason school hallways tend to be so noisy may be the pent-up demand for conversation that has been thwarted by the very structure of the building itself. Exceptions exist, of course. For example, the Illinois Mathematics and Science Academy has several spaces in its building that support conversations. It is common to see students conversing in pairs, working on projects together outside the formalism of a structured classroom (see figure 3.2).

The inclusion of conversational spaces is central to schools designed by the firm of Fielding Nair. A new STEM (science, technology, engineering, and mathematics) magnet school in Michigan City,

Figure 3.2
Source: James Gerry.

Indiana, has conversational spaces designed into the building, but this approach is not taken in the design of many new schools.

The need for conversation seems especially high after a lecture or other formal presentation. Learners are engaged in thinking about what they just saw and heard, and, most naturally, they want to discuss this with others who attended the same event. Note that this is completely different from a formal question-and-answer period after a speech—it entails the kinds of dialogue around a common theme in which the presenter may even gather new insights into his or her own work.

You have probably attended speeches at which the presenter asks you to discuss something with the person next to you for two minutes, after which you share what you've learned with the group. Although this may be a bit productive, it in no way substitutes for the time needed to engage in deeper conversations about a topic. Think about a dinner party. Guests arrive, get introduced to any new people in attendance, and then engage in "small talk" until dinner is served. The small talk is sometimes much more than that. Such conversations help build an understanding and appreciation for the other people in attendance—and all this takes place without an agenda or theme.

In school, themes are important. Approaches to solving a tricky calculus problem or exploring the concept of angular momentum lend themselves to conversational learning just as well as any other topic one might imagine. And conversational learning takes place at all ages. Watch five-year-olds during recess or snack time—they are engaged in dialogues, all facilitated by themselves with no outside intervention needed. The human need and capacity for dialogue-based learning is innate. It is probably in our DNA as a species.

If you need more evidence, look (as we will in some detail later) at technology use. There are over 6 billion cell phones in use, and only 1.6 billion television sets.[4] Televisions are didactic campfires whose glow comes from a screen. Telephones are conversational tools. The huge gap between cell phone adoption and television use is not only staggering, but it also provides further confirmation that dialogue among peers is important for learning.

Our educational institutions should reflect this in their design, but even without new designs, educators should keep this in mind when planning their lessons and be sure to organize time for students to have real conversations about the material they're studying.

CHAPTER 4

Caves

The next learning space on our list is the Cave—the home to reflective learning. This process is solitary and involves self-directed meaning making that can be facilitated with outside resources (books, online informational services, etc.). If the Campfire is home to the lecture, and the Watering Hole is home to the dialogue, the Cave is home to the cognitive construction of understanding of the sort described by Jean Piaget.[1] Unlike the social constructivism of Vygotsky, the cognitive constructivism of Piaget is largely a personal act, although it is informed by presentations and conversations. The point here is for the learner to internalize what he or she knows through experimenting and reflecting on observations.

There are two key Piagetian principles for teaching and learning:

- *Learning is an active process:* Direct experience, making errors, and looking for solutions are vital for the assimilation and accommodation of information. When information is provided through the strategies of problem solving, for example, this is far different from the traditional presentation of arbitrary "facts." Similar to powerful conversations, it is hard, if not impossible, to fit this activity into a specific period of time.
- *Learning should be whole, authentic, and "real":* Meaning is constructed as children interact in powerful ways with the world around them. The focus needs to be on whole activities as opposed to isolated skill exercises.

As my friend Jim Brazell told me years ago, context—not content—is king. With the explosive rise of the infosphere, we are drowning in information. The last thing we need is to pump even more of it into the heads of learners. Making meaning from this information—the development of understanding—is what we really should be teaching. In the Piagetian model, learning is contextual.

As the poet Edna St. Vincent Millay wrote in "Sonnet X":

> Upon this gifted age, in its dark hour,
> Rains from the sky a meteoric shower
> Of facts . . . they lie unquestioned, uncombined.
> Wisdom enough to leech us of our ill
> Is daily spun; but there exists no loom
> To weave it into fabric.[2]

If there was a meteoric shower of facts in 1939 when this poem was published, we can only wonder what she would think of the Internet today! But if the goal is to weave these facts into wisdom, this brings the importance of Piaget's ideas to the forefront.

In thinking about this topic some years ago, I suggested that there were four domains of importance: Data, Information, Knowledge, and Understanding. A goal of education is to help learners move from Data to Understanding, but this process is not a linear one. Consider figure 4.1.

This schematic shows the four domains from Data to Understanding and the various connections between them. The path to Understanding is far from a single straight line. You might start with some

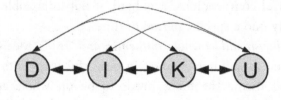

Figure 4.1

raw Data that you are able to turn into Information. On the road to Knowledge, you might find that you need more Data or more Information. The same is true for Understanding. The process of developing Understanding in any domain is highly iterative and nonlinear. Cave work involves the kind of deep and prolonged thought and research needed to build a personal understanding of a domain of inquiry.

A challenge faced in many educational settings is that some learners may claim they *understand* something that they simply *know*. For example, they may know the Pythagorean theorem but not understand it well enough to know why it is true or to develop a proof of it from first principles.

So what kind of space is the Cave? It is clearly a reflective space and, depending on the learner, it may be a solitary one. Perhaps it is like the tree under which Newton was sitting when an apple fell on his head and he realized that the force pulling an apple to earth was universally applicable to all objects, including the planets. As described in a biography of Newton based on interviews and published in 1752.

> After dinner, the weather being warm, we went into the garden and drank tea, under the shade of some apple trees . . . he told me, he was just in the same situation, as when formerly, the notion of gravitation came into his mind. It was occasion'd by the fall of an apple, as he sat in contemplative mood. Why should that apple always descend perpendicularly to the ground, thought he to himself.[3]

The story of Newton seeing the apple fall is probably one of the most famous stories ever told about the history of science. The fact that the experience leading to this profound discovery was a result of the Cave is significant. In today's hectic life, there is precious little time for quiet contemplation, yet, as Newton found, it is through such contemplation that some of the greatest discoveries are made. We should ask what the consequences are for a society that doesn't value the kind of thinking that takes place during quiet periods of reflection. As my friend Prasad Kaipa once said to me, "We have become human doings, not human beings." Yes, the doing part is very important (as we explore in chapter 5), but in order for us to advance and share our ideas we need to have them first.

In many ways, Cave time is the hardest to understand. If you are engaged in quiet reflection on a topic, others may think you aren't working or are daydreaming on the job. This is why I always liked having offices with doors that closed so I could cocoon myself from the outside world when puzzling my way through a particularly nasty problem. I find it interesting that hotel rooms have "do not disturb" signs, but most offices do not. The situation is even worse in classrooms where thirty students or more may be packed like sardines with little to no chance for privacy. Schools that still have libraries afford some places for quiet reflection in many cases. One such library at the high school in Michigan City, Indiana, was even thinking of extending its hours and adding a coffee shop. The only thing holding this back is the large number of students reliant on school buses to get them home. Add to this the plethora of after-school activities that fill up the days of many students, and it is a wonder they get time to think and reflect at all.

Have you ever had the experience of someone interrupting your quiet reflection by saying, "Hey, hope you don't mind, but I wanted to talk with you now that you're not busy." The idea that learning requires activity that can always be observed by others is wrong but one that seems culturally ingrained. Some schools provide quiet rooms but typically only for the primary grades, not for everyone. The apparent belief is that a student is sleeping or is doing something not related to learning if he is too quiet. And to be fair, given our traditional teaching methodologies, this may well be the case.

CAVES IN ACTION

A beautiful example of a school-based Cave can be found at the Poughkeepsie Day School, designed by Fielding Nair International (see figure 4.2).

Figure 4.2

This school is one of many designed with special spaces for different kinds of learning. Students are free to migrate from one environment to another as they need to work on their projects. Unlike the one-size-fits-all model, this school honors the integrity of children and their innate capacity to be amazing learners.

THE CHALLENGE

The problem is not just providing reflective time or special spaces, it is giving students something to reflect *on*. Just as changing the practice of educators takes time, so does getting students to modify their behavior. Typically, Cave time in a learning setting results in some students realizing they do not understand some of the core concepts they thought they knew. For example, if students are given a good block of time to work on a project, they may use some of that time in reflection. When I have done robotics workshops with middle school kids, they have plenty of time to reflect and invent an approach to a challenge I gave them before they start building something. If they are having trouble, it is time for them to emerge from the Cave and resolve these misunderstandings through interaction with their peers (Watering Hole), or, if everyone is having problems, a brief presentation to the class by the teacher (Campfire).

I want to wrap up our introduction to the Cave with a personal story that involved me falling asleep. Many years ago, when my son was an infant, I took care of him at night. One night I was awakened from a good sleep by the sound that meant "I need my diaper changed." I wiped the sleep from my eyes and went in to take care of him, still half-asleep at the time. While I was there I had an insight that (at the time) I was convinced was the most important idea I had ever had. I grabbed the cardboard top off a box of disposable diapers and drew a diagram. After that I went back to sleep.

The next morning I looked at what I had drawn and was puzzled (see figure 4.3).

The drawing showed what appeared to be a current source attached to a tapered element that I assumed was resistive (what we later called *tapered resistors*). After puzzling over this drawing it occurred to me that when electrical current flowed through this device, the narrow region would heat up more than the wider part. If the surface of this

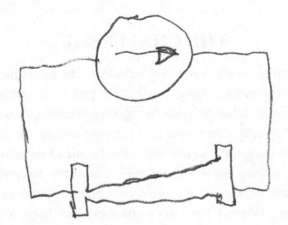

Figure 4.3

device was coated with a material that changed color at a certain temperature (like some liquid crystal materials available at the time), then the length of the visible line would be proportional to the current flowing through the device. In other words, this was an electrical meter with no moving parts that could be built for pennies.

I went to my lab and, within a day or two, had a working prototype in my hands. Although this was not a life-changing invention, I thought it was pretty cool and was granted a patent on it a few years later.[4]

Many years later these devices started showing up on Duracell batteries to allow purchasers to check battery freshness. Millions of people were able to benefit from an insight I had in the Cave. Who knows what great ideas *you* can find in your own private reflective space!

In schools, Cave time probably represents the greatest challenge to the transformation of curriculum, but the Cave is essential in our toolbox of learning spaces and should not be overlooked. Now that we are seeing the disastrous consequences of our focus on education as test preparation, new standards have been written to reflect the idea that learning takes place in many ways. We have replaced a curriculum that is a mile wide and an inch deep with one that digs more deeply into a few core concepts. For example, one of the core curricular ideas in the Next Generation Science Standards is "energy." Energy shows up in many scientific and engineering disciplines and can be explored in multiple ways. When students are presented with questions as the triggers for learning, it is appropriate and productive for students to reflect on the problem and possible solutions before jumping into finding a solution. The challenge, though, is that educators need to realize that this kind of reflective thought is essential to the problem-solving process and to build it into the school day.

CHAPTER 5

Life

How do we know that we know what we know? This seemingly philosophical question can serve as a good starting point for this chapter in which I suggest that our true knowledge is demonstrated in a publicly shared artifact created by the person or group interested in establishing his or her (or their) true knowing.

In the context of our four learning spaces, Life is the one devoted to the meaningful application of the things learned. Through this application comes either demonstration of the depth of the knowledge or the realization that things were not understood as well as first thought, requiring more work on the learner's part. If the Watering Hole is home to Vygotsky's social constructivism, and the Cave is home to Piaget's cognitive constructivism, then Life is home to what Seymour Papert calls *constructionism*. As he and coauthor Idit Harel state,

> It is easy enough to formulate simple catchy versions of the idea of constructionism; for example, thinking of it as "learning-by-making." One purpose of this introductory chapter is to orient the reader toward using the diversity in the volume to elaborate—to construct—a sense of constructionism much richer and more multifaceted, and very much deeper in its implications, than could be conveyed by any such formula.
>
> My little play on the words "construct" and "constructionism" already hints at two of these multiple facets—one seemingly

"serious" and one seemingly "playful." The serious facet will be familiar to psychologists as a tenet of the kindred, but less specific, family of psychological theories that call themselves "contructivist." Constructionism—the N word as opposed to the V word—shares constructivism's connotation of learning as "building knowledge structures" irrespective of the circumstances of the learning. It then adds the idea that this happens especially felicitously in a context where the learner is consciously engaged in constructing a public entity, whether it's a sand castle on the beach or a theory of the universe. And this in turn implies a ramified research program which is the real subject of this introduction and of the volume itself. But in saying all this I must be careful not to transgress the basic tenet shared by the V and the N forms: If one eschews pipeline models of transmitting knowledge in talking among ourselves as well as in theorizing about classrooms, then one must expect that I will not be able to tell you my idea of constructionism. Doing so is bound to trivialize it. Instead, I must confine myself to engage you in experiences (including verbal ones) liable to encourage your own personal construction of something in some sense like it. Only in this way will there be something rich enough in your mind to be worth talking about.[1]

It is important to note that through constructionism the learner not only demonstrates the learning that has taken place but also continues the learning process simply by virtue of building, tinkering, and sharing the construction with others. Speaking for myself, it is through this domain that I learned most effectively because it allowed me to tie together the fragments I had picked up in the other three learning spaces.

For example, in high school I was taught about Gay-Lussac's law—that the pressure of a gas in a closed container increases with the temperature. A friend and I decided to check this out by putting a small carbon dioxide cylinder (the kind used to make sparkling water) in a vise and then heating the canister with a blow torch. Before long, the pressure had increased so much the metal plug at the lip of the cylinder blew out, and the cylinder itself shot free of the vise, blew through the wall of his house, and became lodged in a tree in his back yard. No one was hurt, although my friend, Mike, had some explaining to do when his folks came home (I believe he attributed the hole to mice).

Of course not all constructions are dangerous, nor should they be. I mention the story only to provide an extreme example.

A different perspective is provided by Gever Tulley in his book *Fifty Dangerous Things.*[2] He argues that the learning that comes through tinkering is extremely important. Toward that end, he has fostered the creation of summer week-long Tinkering Schools, and has founded a K–12 school in San Francisco called Brightworks, also based on some of the same principles.[3] Central to the Brightworks pedagogy is the concept of the arc:

> Each arc takes as its premise a central theme, to be explored from multiple perspectives. Students interact with this theme in three different phases: exploration, expression, and exposition. In short, the exploration phase involves tinkering with ideas with the goal of solving a particular problem—for example, building a boat that can carry two people using only scrap materials. Once a suitable plan has been devised, the ideas are expressed through the building of the vessel, and the exposition involves demonstrating the finished project in a real-world situation.[4]

Unlike traditional schools that focus on the Campfire, the Brightworks model is focused on the learning space of Life. In my view, a more balanced approach is likely to be most effective because all four learning spaces connect to help learners build understanding, but it is refreshing to see that someone has responded to the challenge of traditional education in such creative ways.

What can traditional schools do to incorporate more of the application (constructionist) space of Life? In contrast to structured labs where students are all given the same task to perform (often demonstrated in detail by the teacher first), a constructionist space affords more freedom to explore and experiment. Students needing help should have it available, but largely they should be allowed to pursue projects on their own. Of course, finding space for this kind of activity can be quite a challenge for schools. But not all projects require physical space—the space can be more conceptual as long as students are granted the freedom to work on these ideas on their own. As for curricular connections, a physics project about angular momentum might result in the construction of a simple device in which objects are connected to a spindle with string, and the student observes the angle between the string and the spindle for different rotational speeds. If there is no room to do this in class, students can be encouraged to create their machines at home and then bring them to school to demonstrate what they found.

Think about the schools you've attended. They probably had libraries, but they probably didn't have shops (unless you were at a career academy where you would find both). Furthermore, imagine the outrage that would accompany any pressure to close a library at your school. Would that same outrage be expressed at the closure of a shop? Probably not. With few exceptions, shops primarily are found in vocational schools, where they serve a purpose far beyond preparing students for jobs right out of school. I was fortunate to attend a vocational school that also had a college-prep program, which meant that some of my classes were "hands-based" and the rest were "head-based." My high school was the second oldest school in Chicago, named after its founder, Albert G. Lane. Mr. Lane was a colleague of Francis Parker, who ran the lab school at the University of Chicago in the 1860s (and for whom an excellent private school is named). Both Lane and Parker were progressive educators influenced by the ideas of John Dewey and others. Whereas Parker focused on academic schools, Lane wanted to build a school that provided a strong academic program along with shop skills so students could enter the world of work directly from graduation. The curriculum provided close ties between subjects (what we call *transferable skills* today). For example, every student studied mechanical drawing and then took a course in plane geometry. Suddenly the shapes used in drawings could be understood in greater depth with the addition of formal geometry. This transdisciplinary approach was still in place when I attended Lane in the late 1950s and early 1960s. Because my personal passion was electronics, I took every course on the subject that Lane offered. On graduation, I worked for a while and then attended Northwestern University, where I was enrolled in a program on electrical engineering. Unfortunately, I already knew the core concepts of electrical engineering, and was one of the few freshmen who had actually used a soldering iron. I changed majors so I could learn something new.

I had chosen to explore electronics at Lane because of my personal interest in the subject (which I retain today). I had no idea we were learning things that were considered core subjects at the university level. So much for the idea that my school was just preparing me for technical work after graduation. In fact, I was miles ahead of my colleagues who attended fine, but purely academic, high schools.

The reality is that shop space in traditional academic schools is hard to find. Some schools have addressed this by building "makerspaces" in their libraries or, if lucky, a room dedicated to the purpose. The key is that the space can adapt to a wide variety of uses and can be shaped by educational purposes as well as the students' creative goals. Ideally this space would be standalone—a room or shed on the school grounds, but this is not always possible. Those interested can learn more about building their own makerspace in *The Makerspace Playbook*,[5] and there will be much more to say on this topic in a later chapter.

The motivation behind the makerspace movement is simple: it is a mind-set based on the idea that we are all makers, not just thinkers, and we need places to invent, work with our heads *and* hands, and build concrete artifacts that can be shared with others. Makers believe that if you can imagine it, you can make it. They see themselves as more than consumers—they are productive; they are creative.

Everyone is a maker, and our world is what we make it. As we will explore in chapter 10, the maker movement is spurred by the introduction of new technologies such as 3D printing and the Arduino microcontroller. Although this chapter, along with those before it, has focused on a single learning space, our perspective is that it is through the blending of all four spaces that education can be most effective and rewarding to students and educators alike. But these learning spaces transcend physical places. They apply to our use of technology as well, and this is the subject of the next section of this book.

CHAPTER 6

The Challenge of Technology

I named the first book on this topic *Campfires in Cyberspace* for a reason. My premise was that for thousands of years people had learned around the campfire, and now that the campfire was being replaced by the glow of a computer monitor, we needed to ensure that the stories told around the new fire were as compelling as those told around the old one.

Of course, technology use as tools for learning is not restricted to didactic (Campfire) presentation of material—all four learning spaces can (and should) be involved in effective technology use in education. The real challenge is not the application of modern technological tools to the four learning spaces, but in keeping up with the never-ending development of new technologies that can be useful in an educational setting, and designing ways to use them to enhance learning.

In this chapter we'll explore this topic from the perspective of 2013, with the full expectation that specific technologies considered cutting edge at the time this is being written may be eclipsed by even more powerful technologies in the future. The goal here is to explore basic principles of technology use that will transcend the development of ever newer, cheaper, and more powerful tools.

TECHNOLOGY IN GENERAL

As mentioned in the first chapter of this book, modern technology can be used to replicate educational practices of the past—amplifying strategies that have never worked for all learners but implementing them with new technologies. This is why, for years, I've argued that we should use the new tools to do different things, not just to do old things differently. The consequences of not doing this are sad on two fronts: first, they tie up scarce resources in the replication of outmoded practices, and, second, they make it harder to "do the right thing." As Jason Ohler says, "Committing a bad story to digital media is like giving a bad guitar player a bigger amplifier."[1] Let's start by looking at interactive whiteboards. This technology had become so popular by 2012, it existed in a huge number of classrooms all over the world. The idea behind the technology was that by connecting computers to display boards, teachers could present material in new ways. Instead of drawing a triangle by hand, it could now be drawn automatically on the board using a projected image on an interactive surface. By using a special pen, or even one's finger, objects could be placed, lines drawn, text added—basically making it easier and cleaner for teachers to present material they would otherwise have to re-create by hand for each class. Images could even be prepared ahead of time and stored on the computer, ready for instant use when the class entered the room. So far, this all sounds pretty interesting, so what is the problem? The problem, quite simply, is that this technology operates on the assumption that the best way for students to learn is for teachers to stand and deliver presentations. If you have gotten this far in this book, you already know how flawed an assumption I think this is. Yet interactive whiteboards are not only commonplace, they are also eagerly embraced by educators who find that it makes their lives easier. Rarely does the topic of appropriateness even come up.

An even worse example of a popular technology is the "clicker," a hand-held remote control with which a student can key in answers to multiple choice questions whose results are displayed on a projection screen (or interactive whiteboard). Built around the laudable idea of getting every child to participate in class activities, this device can provide a safe way for students to answer questions in class without fear of ridicule by their peers if they get the wrong answer. And, again, it is logical to ask, what is wrong with this? The downside in this case is that it is designed on the assumption that student responses take the form of answers to closed questions, which lend themselves to being answered in a multiple-choice format. This has the effect of turning student interaction into a TV game show— a potentially enjoyable activity sadly devoid of good educational practice.

For example, a clicker question might be, "What is the capital of California?" with four or five possible responses, only one of which is correct. Consider the difference between this and the following question: "Why is Sacramento the capital of California?" This open-ended question can lead to robust historical research in which students learn that the capital city has had different locations since the state was founded, and also they can find the motivation for selecting the current capital city. Obviously, this is a far richer experience for learners, and one that is too often closed off in a classroom where clickers and the didactic presentation of material are dominant.

In short, saying that technology is being used in a classroom conveys nothing of value without elaboration. The tools used to perpetuate the past are most easily adopted because they require no real transformation on the part of the educators. They simply put a fresh face on strategies that have been known to fail to reach all learners since 1350.

TECHNOLOGICAL CHANGE

Another challenge regarding technology is the speed with which it changes. One of McLuhan's great contributions was the understanding that every technology does four things: it does something new, it replaces something old, it rekindles something from the past, and it sets the stage for its own obsolescence by flipping into something else.[2]

For example, let's look at the word processor. When word processors came out, they allowed people to create nicely formatted documents without having to use typesetting equipment. Ultimately this made it easier for people to publish their own work, whether it was an article or a book. This clearly was something new. As for replacing something old, the typewriter has fallen from use since word processing software became commonplace. This happened for several reasons, chief among them being the ease with which documents could be edited without having to type them all over again. As for rekindling something from the past, word processing software rekindled an interest in typographic design, something that had been developed by printers since the 1500s and, especially, through the work of Aldus Manutius whose *italic* type is still commonplace today. Many popular typefaces are based on those developed many hundreds of years ago. Consider Palatino, for example. Named after 16th-century Italian master of calligraphy, Giambattista Palatino, the modern Palatino typeface is based on the humanist fonts of the Italian Renaissance, which mirror the letters formed by a broad-nib pen. This gives a calligraphic grace to the letters and makes them quite legible. The ability to choose among multiple fonts was largely unknown to those who used typewriters. In fact, once people started using word processors instead of typewriters, it was common to see so many typefaces being used that documents started looking more like ransom notes until people realized that with freedom comes responsibility, and typographic elegance became the norm for most people.

The real challenge in McLuhan's tetrad is figuring out what comes next. What does the new technology flip into? In the case of word processing, one possible flip was the rise of interactive multimedia—something that required a computer and could not be done on a typewriter. Of course, this part of the tetrad is easy to see in hindsight. The challenge is to see what is coming next when the topic of exploration is, itself, a fairly new technology. As an old friend once cautioned me, "Watch out, David, those who live by the crystal ball shall eat crushed glass." This was good advice, but it doesn't keep me from trying to anticipate the future anyway.

Some technologies are easy to forecast—for example, those driven by evolutionary forces such as Moore's Law. In its current form, this law states that the complexity (and power) of microprocessors, for example, doubles every year, and the cost goes down. We see this played out every time new computers come on the market, and are no longer surprised when our current computers suddenly seem old and out-of-date. But there are other forces for change, and some of these cannot be anticipated. We call these changes *wild cards* because they show up by surprise. Consider the transistor—a device invented in 1947 that had the potential to eclipse the vacuum tube in everything from radios to computers. When transistors came to market, they were, in fact, inferior to vacuum tubes, but their rapid improvement and adoption made vacuum tube–based devices virtually obsolete and opened the door to the invention of the integrated circuit and the modern laptop. The inability to see the future resulted in some quotes that look pretty silly today. For example, consider this quote from *Popular Mechanics* in 1949 (two years after the invention of the transistor): "Computers in the future may weigh no more than 1.5 tons."[3] When this was written, the Eniac had been built. This first true digital computer occupied an entire room, making the *Popular Mechanics* prediction sound amazing. But no one seemed to realize that the days of vacuum tube technology were numbered, being driven out by the invention of a new device whose features and capabilities had already been demonstrated.

There are numerous examples of when people got it wrong because they simply extrapolated from the past without being aware of the coming disruption caused by the wild card aspect of some emerging technologies.

And, to make things even more interesting, the rate of technological change today seems to be accelerating. Futurists used to be thrilled
when they could forecast developments five years out. Today, if lucky,
the period is more like one year.

These observations should be taken as a caveat for our application
of technology to learning spaces. McLuhan's model shows that technology is on an ever-advancing path. There are many driving forces
for change, but change itself is inevitable and rapid. No doubt you
will see examples in this and later chapters as some of the tools we
describe have either morphed into new forms or have disappeared
altogether.

EDUCATION'S RESPONSE TO NEW TECHNOLOGIES

If the forces that drive the creation of new technology are strong, the
resistance to the adoption of some of these tools is even stronger,
especially if the new tools are in conflict with the dominant educational paradigm. For example, students have long brought cell phones,
digital gaming tools, and other personal devices into the classroom,
but the use of these devices was forbidden for the overt reason that
they may open the door to "cheating," and for the covert reason they
would trigger a change in pedagogical practice. Evidence of this resistance has appeared all around the world, but finally the pressure
brought by students was too much to withstand, at least in many
schools, as evidenced by this headline from the October 12, 2010,
issue of the *Chicago Tribune:* "After years of banning hand-held
devices, many high-schools are conceding defeat, allowing them to be
used as academic tools."[4]

Wow! Look at the language: "conceding defeat" speaks volumes
about the forces aligned against the use of student-owned devices in
the classroom! In my presentations and workshops I asked teachers
to explain their misgivings—and the most common response was that

students would use their hand-held devices to look up answers to test questions. My response was to suggest that this could be solved by asking questions for which Google is not the answer. Of course, this is easier said than done.

Recall, a few chapters back, we explored the idea that there were four levels of learning—Data, Information, Knowledge, and Understanding. Although there is an implied hierarchy, the process of moving between levels is interactive. One may find, for example, that the advancement from knowledge to understanding might require gathering more Data first. The first two of these (Data and Information) are readily addressed by Google. Suppose we were to just acknowledge this and concentrate on the higher forms of Knowledge and Understanding. These are the areas of most interest to students and educators alike. Of course, they cannot be addressed without the requisite Data and Information, and this suggests where we can create a synergy between student-owned devices and the curriculum. It is clear that student-owned devices are not going away any time soon—and in fact they are growing in number and capability—so let's think about ways to use them effectively in schools.

Not all schools share this belief. Schools in New York still ban cell phones, forcing kids to store them in trucks outside the school for a dollar a day.[5] Attempts by the city council to change this were squashed by Mayor Bloomberg. And New York is not alone. I trust that one day soon this nonsense will get resolved and we can celebrate the educational power of devices students carry with them every day.

TABLET COMPUTERS IN THE CLASSROOM

Rather than spend more time exploring inappropriate technology use, I want to continue this overview section with a brief examination of tablet computing, because these devices, along with smartphones, are the basis for the movement toward bring-your-own-device policies in schools across the world.

From a historical perspective, the move to bring computing to all students has failed. Yes, some schools implemented one-to-one programs around laptops, often with great success, but this trend did not spread to all schools, even as the price of personal technologies dropped to the point that we could purchase a laptop computer for all students at a fraction of the cost of textbooks. Of course, this assumes that schools stop squandering their money on textbooks. Taking a paper book and putting it online does nothing to improve pedagogical practice. It is time to let go of the idea that textbooks help develop the habits of mind that will last students for a lifetime. Whether the reluctance to adopt ubiquitous computing came from the fear that it would make current teacher-centric practices obsolete, or required too many changes in the infrastructure of schools, the fact remains that such programs were few and far between. (By the way, for those who still want textbooks, an amazingly accurate collection is available from www.ck12.org).

But, outside of school, smartphones and other personal information devices are increasingly being purchased by students or their families, and are being brought into the classroom where students expect to be able to use them for educational purposes.[6] The global growth of cell phone use is nothing short of astonishing. By the end 2012 there were about six billion cell phones in the world. And the growth has not stopped. Old cell phones designed to simply make phone calls are being replaced at a prodigious rate by smartphones—devices that not only make phone calls but also run a plethora of applications, many of which can be used effectively in an educational setting. Google's Android operating system for mobile devices, with 72 percent of the market, is growing at about 1.3 million devices per day, every day of the week.[7]

Edward R. Murrow famously stated that "television is the world's largest classroom."[8] Although the educational potential of television may have been true at the time he said this (Murrow saw it as a failed revolution), it is no longer the case even if television *had* lived up to its promise. Contrast the 6 billion cell phones with the 1.4 billion televisions in the world, and the scope of the new revolution becomes clear. Interactive mobile technologies have far eclipsed passive televisions, and our students have these new devices with them all the time.

The rise of the tablet computer has been interesting to watch. Unlike the computer battles, which focused on Microsoft and Apple, the world of tablets has now shaped up as a battle between Google and Apple, with Microsoft playing (in mid-2013) a relatively insignificant role.

But there is more that distinguishes these devices than a difference in operating systems. There is, in fact, a fundamentally different philosophy between the two companies with respect to how devices based on their platforms should be used. Because this difference in philosophy has an impact on how the respective platforms might be used in education, it is worth spending a few minutes on the topic. Apple created an elegant device, the iPad, that defined the original tablet use in the United States. All software for these devices (applications, or *apps*) is made available through the Apple store after being reviewed and accepted for the market. Android apps, however, can be made available through the Google store, or can be created, downloaded, and installed by users directly without having to thread one's way through the censor's needle. It is, as one blogger put it, like the difference between a highly packaged and structured vacation through the medium of a traditional cruise or Club Med and booking your own vacation and going where you want when you want.[9] It is not that one is better than the other. There is a reason both options exist, and they each have their place. The challenge is that in education it comes down to the difference between choosing a tool largely used for the consumption of information (the iPad) or a tool of creation (Android devices). Yes, both can be used as electronic textbooks (one of those ways of preserving the past while creating the illusion of newness), and they can both be used for the creation of simple documents, picture editing, and so on. And, as HTML5 becomes more commonplace, web-based apps that run equally well on both platforms will blur the distinctions even more. But, for now, if you want students to be able to use their devices to, for example, create their own controllers for robotic devices of their own design (a task in the Life space), the choice is clear, and it is not Apple. As for the future, only time will tell.

This was not the case in the personal computer wars. All personal computers, independent of operating systems, could be used as tools of consumption *and* tools of creation. I have no doubt that the same will ultimately be true for tablets, but at this moment your choice of platform for educational use requires some thought that transcends price and other traditional factors.

DEEP CHANGES IN INTERACTION

Although specific technologies come and go, one recent change seems to have taken hold and shows no sign of reverting to the old way of doing things—the move from mouse-based computing to the navigation and activation of tasks through the use of gestures. When my granddaughter, Bianca, was four years old, we were walking in a local park whose office had a computer kiosk showing what plays and musical events were scheduled for the month. She walked up to the kiosk and immediately started wiping the screen with her finger. As she expected, the pages flipped to show other screens. What was interesting to me was how natural the process of using gestures was to her as a way to navigate computer-based information. Of course, she has lots of technology at home, and, although she started her computer experiences using a mouse, she now does almost everything she needs with gestures. For her, these are natural ways of interacting with computers.

On a grander scale, consider the Microsoft Kinect—an interface they designed for the Xbox 360 video game console. This device uses body movement and gestures to control game play without the user having to touch anything at all. With the release of a software developers' kit, it is possible to use this powerful device with ordinary personal computers, and this kind of sophisticated gesture-based interaction is on the way to becoming commonplace.

More recently, the MIT Media Lab announced the LuminAR Project (http://fluid.media.mit.edu/projects/luminar) led by Natan Linder in which a desk lamp has been converted to a gesture-based interactive system. With a built-in video projector and all the sensors needed to interact with the screen, the device can transform any surface into an interactive digital space.

Does this mean that the mouse is dead as a pointing device? Not necessarily—but it is surely declining in terms of its impact. As someone who started in the field when cursor control keys were the norm, I moved to the mouse, the single-touch controller, the multitouch controller, and to purely gesture-based interaction with computers without requiring any touching at all. For children entering school today, the mouse is likely to be as foreign to them as it was in the early 1970s when it was being developed and refined.

TECHNOLOGICAL REVOLUTIONS THAT HAVE HAD A MAJOR IMPACT ON EDUCATION

Does the rapid rise of new technologies mean we can't see long-lasting trends in education driven by the emergence of new tools? Of course not. In fact, from my perspective, there have been three consumer-driven technological revolutions that have rocked education to its core.

The first of these was the invention of the phonetic alphabet, of which the cuneiform representation of Akkadian, developed around 2500 BCE, is a prime example. The power of this representational system is that it allowed multiple languages to be written using a single set of orthographic symbols. The epic of Gilgamesh is a fine example of the kinds of things written using this system.

The second major revolution for education was the rise of the mass-produced modern book—a development attributed to the Venetian humanist and typesetter, Aldus Manutius, in the late 1400s—sixty years after Johannes Gutenberg pioneered the use of movable type. Credited with the invention of the italic typeface and the publishing of compact books with vellum binding—precursors to the modern paperback—Aldus also pioneered the mass production of books. Unlike the previous printing tradition, in which books were made by the copy for a single customer, Aldus published books with press runs ranging from two hundred to one thousand, thus reaching a wide audience and helping the spread of literacy throughout Europe.

And that brings us to today, when the consumer revolution of personal informational devices (smartphones and tablets) demonstrates their power as potential learning tools, even if they (similar to the mass-produced book before them) are resisted by the educational establishment.

WHAT THE FUTURE HOLDS

As for the future, I have no idea what amazing new devices will show up for use in educational settings. I do feel confident, however, that some of these tools will be adopted based on their ability to help preserve the failed pedagogical paradigms of the past, and others will open the doors to a new kind of education—one that honors the diversity of learning strategies associated with the four learning spaces described in this book.

Keeping in mind that social change has always lagged technological change, I remain optimistic that our technological tools will be used in ways that improve education for everyone, but ultimately that task falls to those of you in the classroom.

We now turn to specific examples of technology use associated with our four metaphorical learning spaces. These examples can all be implemented using readily available tools found in schools, homes, and even student backpacks. As you explore these examples, you are likely to think of other and even newer technologies that might fit into one of the four categories we've defined.

CHAPTER 7

Technological Campfires

The domain of technology use in educational Campfires is probably the most fully developed and is surely the most popular among educators. Whether through e-books or through video lectures provided by (for example) the Khan Academy (www.khanacademy.org), educators are scrambling to take advantage of these tools whenever they can. The Khan Academy has more than three thousand video "lessons" online that can be accessed for free by students and educators alike, and has been partly responsible for the idea of the "flipped" classroom, in which the homework consists of attending the online lectures, freeing class time for teachers to work with students to help grow and cement the things they have learned. By moving "homework" into the classroom, and leaving the lectures to be seen at home, students are provided with content area assistance that is (generally) greater than that provided by parents—or at least so goes the rationale. Flipped classrooms are variations of the concept of "blended learning," in which both physical and virtual spaces are used as part of the educational experience.

In fact, blended learning *is* the norm and has been since students gained access to the Internet, even if schools didn't recognize it as such. Most students make extensive use of the web to look up things they aren't clear on—whether it is a historical incident, a rule of grammar, or the proof of the chain rule in calculus. And this research generally takes place outside the classroom.

What goes unanswered in this approach, though, is whether or not lecture-based presentations make sense—independently of whether they are delivered through videos or by face-to-face presentations.

The growth of online resources has also helped drive the movement toward electronic (e-) textbooks. In general, e-books can be downloaded to the student's device and used at any time, even if network access is not available. One argument in favor of e-texts is the fact that they do not add weight to a student's backpack. They also can be updated frequently, because there is no inventory of bound books that needs to be recycled. Although traditional textbook publishers are eager to provide e-books, they generally are equally eager to keep their prices the same as the paper versions, requiring schools to invest heavily in these items to the detriment of other expenditures that might better support the other learning spaces.

One exception to this is the open textbook movement, led by CK–12 (www.cK–12.org). The central idea behind this collection of free textbook materials is their openness. This is reflected through the concept of the "FlexBook." In FlexBooks, individual teachers can assemble their own texts using existing and new modules to craft their own support materials, including video and interactive quizzes. Because the content is open, this level of personalization for educators is unprecedented. So, for example, a teacher of US history who wants to emphasize a subtopic based on her PhD research is free to do so. As for the accuracy of the offerings, FlexBooks were found to be more accurate than textbooks published by traditional publishers in a study done for the State of California.[1]

With the options of online lectures; free, accurate, open-source textbooks; and all the other resources available on the Internet, it would seem that the role of technology in the traditional didactic Campfire space is well established. And if this were the only learning space we used, that would be fine. But effective Campfire practices can also set the stage for activities in the other learning spaces. It is in the synergistic connection between the learning spaces where the greatest power lies, and this is an area that needs more work. For example, in my own teaching at the university level I make heavy use of TED videos (www.ted.com). These short presentations focus on providing challenging ideas and breakthrough thinking. Although they are informational on their own, they also make great spring-boards for rich conversations and, as such, lead the way into other learning spaces (including the Cave and Life). For example, a TED video from a few years back showed that the inexpensive controller from a Wii video game could be used to build a gesture-based controller for a display screen.[2] Within a very short period of time, people were talking with their friends and building their own replicas of this device. The Campfire experience of this shared video led to further activities in the other learning spaces, including discussions at the Watering Hole and the hands-on experimenting in the constructionist space of Life. In my view, we need even more of these kinds of experiences—activities that seamlessly move from one learning space to another in support of a learner's quest for understanding.

FIXING ONE OF THE MAIN PROBLEMS WITH LECTURES

I attended high school with a great guy whose family had emigrated from one of the Eastern Bloc countries in the late 1950s. For my buddy George, English was a confusing second language that he worked very hard to master. Among other things, George loved to tell jokes and, to keep them in his mind, he attached the punch line to the body of the joke—and this came out when he would share his latest acquisition. For example, "What do you call a four-room watermelon that is green on the outside, red on the inside, and houses four people?"

Well, thanks, George, you just told us! We thought it was kind of funny how he stored material in his mind, but it never occurred to us that our teachers were doing the same thing—putting the punch line of their lesson into the lecture.

If the teacher is going to tell everything without being prompted, then why should a student pay attention? What part of a typical school lecture stimulates real thinking or problem solving or research? For that matter, how does a teacher's lecture spark any real interest in the subject—an interest that could trigger a career choice for some students?

Campfire-based tools can be of great value as we make the pedagogical shift toward a more project-based learning (PBL) approach to education. The fact is that inquiry-driven PBL can be a challenge for teachers and students alike. From the teacher's perspective, there is the temptation to reveal more information than needed to students as they are launched on their projects—to incorporate the punch line into the lecture. From the students' point of view, they have become so used to all the relevant information coming either from the teacher's mouth, or from a canned source of information such as that found in textbooks, that they don't know how to make the transition to thinking for themselves.

Once education is viewed from a PBL perspective, all this changes, and educators and students need all the help they can get in making the transition. This help can come in the form of a didactic presentation whose goal is not to teach an entire concept, but designed instead to set the stage for student exploration (and learning) of the topic on her own.

Fortunately there is a solution—a way to give presentations without revealing the punch line.

THE KNIGHTS OF KNOWLEDGE

In the 1990s, in an attempt to build bridges for educators interested in inquiry, my wife, Norma, and I created a fictional ancient organization called the *Knights of Knowledge*. Students were told that this group was founded in antiquity and included Socrates, Pythagoras, Archimedes, Newton, Galileo, Madame Curie, Pablo Picasso, Stravinsky, Georgia O'Keefe, Roger Bannister, and numerous others up to modern times. Those selected for this secret organization had two characteristics: first, they asked and then answered interesting questions. Second, each answer led to even more interesting questions.

Our reason for creating this fictional society was based on the observation that children love the idea of being involved in something secret and special. And so they were told that the Knights of Knowledge needs new members, and its leader has created a subgroup called the *Special Agents*. Students are invited to join the Special Agents and are presented with short video-based presentations setting up a compelling question that forms the basis of an in-depth research project related to the curriculum. (For examples of the videos, see the Knights of Knowledge website: http://knights-of-knowledge.com/projects .html.) Each video clip is only a minute or so in length—just long enough to set the stage for the challenge and ask the question. From then on, the student is on his or her own to find answers and build a report before generating follow-on questions. For example, the question might relate to the observation that some trees change colors in the fall and then drop their leaves, yet other trees keep their leaves all year long. Then they are asked why that is. Another project might relate to the observation that we measure time in units of sixty (for seconds and minutes), not one hundred, and then ask why this is. To the extent possible, the questions are deep enough to require some significant research to answer—not just a quick copy of something from a Google search.

Nearly any subject at any grade and in any content area is ripe for the generation of questions that can be used to stimulate student research. Our observation was that once a question was posed, it automatically led to other questions generated by students as they completed their project.

For example, one video we made showed a photograph of a church built in Portugal during the late Middle Ages. This church was heavily fortified, and the goal was to explain why churches built in that period needed fortification. No mention of the Moors was made in the video, and this became something the students would find out about on their own. In researching the history of the period, some students might come across the observation that in Cordova, Spain, Muslims, Catholics, and Jews lived in harmony—a topic that might not show up in the traditional world-history curriculum. And this, of course, leads to the further question of why that happened, why the situation seems different today, and what we might do to change that. In short, myriad questions can erupt from a project triggered by comments on a few photographs of a Portuguese church.

Each project can run from one class period to several days depending on the depth of the inquiry done by the students. We've even designed projects that last an entire term. We propose that teachers new to the process start out with one- or two-period activities and then move on to providing more time for students to explore topics in greater detail.

When students are researching topics on their own, there is a huge opportunity for them to develop passion for the subject area—a passion that does not appear in traditional textbook approaches to instruction. This passion is, in my view, essential in education. Too many of our courses are "about" topics. We teach children about history, about mathematics, about biology, but not enough attention is paid to getting them to think like historians, mathematicians, or biologists. How can we expect to attract children into any of the professions if we don't help them see how people working in these fields think and solve problems—and find their work compelling?

CONTENT AREA MODULES THAT CROSS DISCIPLINES AND GRADE LEVELS

Each Knights of Knowledge quest is based on material germane to at least one subject area, with the likelihood that multiple subjects will be involved in the project. This builds transferability across domains, a major skill described in the new standards and not addressed in many textbook-driven approaches of the past. For example, one mission might ask why the numbers 5, 8, 13, 21, and so on show up so often in plants. For example, the number of intersecting spirals on pineapples have these numbers. A very large number of flowers have five petals, and Fibonacci numbers (numbers following the series 1, 2, 3, 5, 8, 13, 21, etc.) show up in the pattern of leaves as they appear on a stem. This activity incorporates math (the Fibonacci series) and plant morphology at the same time.

The quests are based on questions that are designed to stimulate student thought. Although some of what they have learned in class may (and should) apply, they will move beyond this content as they explore it more deeply.

Here are a few questions that span the curriculum:

- How can you tell in advance what color a leaf will turn in the fall? (This project leads to experimentation and involves several disciplines, including biology and the physics of osmosis.)
- Why does time get measured in units of sixty instead of one hundred (seconds, minutes)? (This project has more to do with history than with mathematics or physics.)
- Why do so many flowers have five petals—and why do the intersecting spirals on a pineapple have the numbers they have? (These projects involve mathematics as well as the morphology of plants.)
- How important is a shared base of core stories and myths to understanding other people as they speak? (A project like this cuts across multiple disciplines—history, language arts, and others.)
- You can completely fill a surface with regular polygons with three, four, and six sides but regular pentagons cannot be used to tile a surface without gaps. Why is that?
- What would have happened in North America if Great Britain had won the Revolutionary War?
- How did birds evolve? (This question leads to explorations in paleontology as well as biology.)

- Why is the land in the states of Illinois, Indiana, Michigan, and Wisconsin so flat whereas the land in Colorado has high mountains?
- What role, if any, did popular music play in bringing an end to the war in Vietnam?

The challenge of creating good driving questions is the subject of workshops we conduct. The goal is to set the stage for you to learn how to build your own questions, from which you can make your own inquiry starters. We provide some resources to help you with this in the next section of this book. Once you start coming up with topics, you may find it hard to stop. Virtually any part of the curriculum is ripe for projects of this type.

Another characteristic of most of the activities based on good driving questions is that they cut across grade levels. The difference lies only in the depth and sophistication of the responses of the students. This also means that these activities are perfect for students ranging from the gifted to the learning challenged.

Note that the videos that go with these projects are very different from instructional videos. The goal is not to teach a specific topic but to provide just enough information to support the development of a compelling question the student will then answer. These videos can be viewed on any device at any time, making this application perfect for use in the flipped classroom, where the challenge is given at home, and school time is used to work on the project. In fact, these videos can redefine the meaning of a flipped classroom in ways that support student engagement, something a video just on fractions could never do.

CREATING YOUR OWN PROJECT VIDEO

If you want to create this kind of video on your own, the task is pretty easy. Production consists of the following:

- Choosing the question
- Writing the script
- Finding or taking images needed in the video
- Building the final video

Let's explore each of these steps in sequence.

Choosing the Question

Of all the tasks, the most important is choosing the question to be explored. We encounter many kinds of questions in life—some with short answers, some with longer answers, and some that have yet to be answered at all. A question such as, "Where is the Iberian Peninsula?" is an example of a short question, and is unworthy of exploration in inquiry-driven PBL. This is an example of the kind of question that can be answered in a few seconds, either from memory or from *Wikipedia*. Education has been focused on these kinds of questions in the past, and it is time to abandon them. With students carrying the Internet in their pockets and backpacks, such questions (without a compelling context) are not interesting.

However, more complex questions (either answerable or not) lend themselves to the kind of deep learning and understanding that is the proper goal of any educational system. Should we ask students to explore questions that have yet to be answered? In my view those are the best kind. The kind of research done in pursuit of such questions mirrors that of people working in the field professionally. And there is the possibility that students might just uncover an approach that the professionals didn't see. You may want to start with questions that are answerable, but as soon as possible, move to the (as yet) unanswerable ones; they are the most exciting.

The kinds of questions I encourage are what the Buck Institute calls *driving questions*.[3] Although examples of good driving questions are not hard to find, they do take some effort. If you are a teacher, you will want to take into consideration four main factors:

- The relevance of the question to the curriculum
- Its capacity to trigger new questions
- Its difficulty (neither too hard nor too easy)
- Its ability to support rich dialogue between students and yourself

A starting point might be with questions you have yourself about the curriculum. For example, if you teach mathematics, you know that a positive times a positive is a positive, a negative times a positive is a negative, and a negative times a negative is a positive. This last observation may seem counterintuitive to your students. What better way to have them grasp the rationale behind this "math fact" than having them research it themselves, perhaps also asking them to describe a real-world situation in which two negative numbers are multiplied together to produce an understandably positive number.

Of course, the same approach can be taken for any subject. Have you ever wondered what the results would be had the Confederacy won the Civil War? If so, let your students run with this problem. Suddenly US history takes on a new perspective when we give ourselves the power to play what-if with reality. Students might learn that isolated events can have huge consequences in the long term, and this might trigger a lifelong love of history!

Writing the Script

Once the driving question is formulated, the next step is to write the script of your video. Most (but not all) of the Knights of Knowledge videos we've created run about a minute in length. They have three components:

- Provide just the right amount of background information to support the driving question.
- State the question.
- Describe the desired format for sharing the results of the inquiry.

For example, consider the following script related to the properties of our moon:

From Earth we enjoy a splendid view of the full moon every twenty-eight days. This view shows some areas with craters, and large darker areas called *maria*, after the Latin word for *seas*. These areas are quite distinctive. But when you look at the far side of the moon—the side not visible from Earth, the image is quite different. There are fewer and smaller maria, and many craters.

Why is this?

Your task is to find the data related to this question, refine it into information, and then demonstrate your knowledge and understanding through the creation of a document or project that can be shared with your colleagues.

This script is quite short, but it contains just enough information to get students started on a well-defined project. It also has the potential to lead to follow-on questions. For example, we only see one side of the moon from Earth, meaning that its revolution around Earth is exactly the same as the period of its rotation. Is this property unique to our moon? Why does it behave this way?

And the questions keep coming . . .

Finding or Taking Images Needed in the Video

Of course you could just give students the problem or record the script as an audio file (using any common audio recording tool such as Audacity [http://audacity.sourceforge.net/download]), but the addition of images helps focus student attention and makes the short presentation more compelling. With a short video, you will not need very many images. Depending on the topic, you can take the images yourself, or you can download them. Be cautious, though, in using downloaded pictures to be sure you are not infringing on someone's copyright! Material from government sites (e.g., NASA, NOAA, etc.) can be used without further permission as long as the source is referenced somewhere. Most images from *Wikipedia* are released under the Creative Commons license, meaning they can be used in your work as well. Where you might run into trouble is using images from Flickr or another image-uploading site. Some people are happy for you to use their work, and others are not. Because your video will only need three or four images, getting good content should not be a big problem.

Building the Final Video

The videos are likely to use a few still images that are provided with effects to give some motion to them as the narration proceeds. As for building the video itself, there are many tools that can be used. One of my favorites is HyperStudio 5 (www.mackiev.com/hyperstudio /index.html). Not only is this tool easy to use, it has the capacity to export your video in a form that lets you post it on sites like YouTube, or, better yet, as an HTML5 or movie file you can post to your own site. This lets the video be seen on any computer or mobile device, including smartphones and tablets. These videos can be watched and rewatched by students as much as they want. In addition to the ability to export finished projects in multiple formats, HyperStudio also provides all the authoring features needed to create your project, including recording of the audio script and the insertion of elegant transitions between images.

THE VALUE OF THE METHOD

As stated previously, one of the immediate values coming from the creation of these videos is that it makes it easy to provide project starters to students without running the risk of giving away the punch line. Furthermore, an archive of these videos can be shared with others, promoting the spread of inquiry-driven PBL far faster than required with traditional staff development methods. Once teachers become comfortable with the process, they will find themselves spending a lot of time writing down the driving questions that pop into their minds automatically! Yes, it requires some work at first, but once you get going, it really takes off!

Our adventure now turns to the application of modern technologies in the domain of the Watering Hole.

●

CHAPTER 8

Technological
Watering Holes

Mention *social learning* in most settings, and people probably think of Facebook. The fact is, although social (Watering Hole) learning doesn't rely on technology, there are many tools (including Facebook) that can be of great utility in this domain. In fact, social learning is probably the original way people learned anything. If it seems we are talking about it more today, this may be simply because of the rise of popularity of social networking tools such as Facebook and Google+ (to name just two) and the increasing extent to which these tools are being used by students and educators alike on a daily basis.

In most educational environments, Watering Hole activities fall under the category of "cooperative learning" in which students work together on a project. This type of learning opens the door to Vygotsky's zone of proximal development and is also a comfortable environment for many students. Unfortunately, the amount of time allocated for collaboration in most classrooms is pretty small. True collaboration in a school setting is not often given much time, and this is a problem that technology can help address.

I remember a few years ago when I was giving a workshop on robotics for students, one of whom was texting in the middle of the workshop. I asked her if everything was OK, and she responded that she had originally planned to go to the shopping center with her friends after school, but signed up for the workshop instead. Her friends were just touching base to see how she was doing and, when she told them, they wanted to know if they could attend the workshop the next time it was offered. Although this was not an educational application of technology, it doesn't take much imagination to see how the same technology could be used in support of learning, and it did serve as a marketing tool for our workshop.

Clare Wood and her colleagues at the University of Coventry have explored texting by nine- and ten-year-old children.[1] They studied 114 children who had never owned a mobile phone before they were recruited, and each child was randomly allocated to either the intervention or control group. All children were pre- and posttested on a range of reading, spelling, and phonological awareness skills. Children in the intervention group were given access to a mobile phone (enabled for text messaging only) for weekends and during half-term break for a ten-week period. The control group did not get mobile phones. It was found that there were no significant statistical differences between the two groups of children in terms of their literacy attainment during that period as measured by traditional examinations. However, within the mobile phone group, there was evidence that use of text abbreviations was positively related to gains in literacy skills in many students. They also found that children's use of textisms (e.g., ROTFL—rolling on the floor laughing) in their messages was positively related to improvement in literacy skills, especially spelling. This counterintuitive result is interesting given the concern that many teachers have that texting will destroy spelling skills! Although it is still the case that many uses of Watering Hole technology are still banned from quite a few schools, outside the classroom most students spend a tremendous amount of time posting on personal blogs, Flickr, YouTube, and other places. They tweet, visit their Facebook page, send text messages, and take part in other technology-mediated activities that make up the category of social networking. The challenge is to see how these tools can be used effectively in an educational setting. One example of how social networking can be used in the classroom is Edmodo (www.edmodo.com), which provides a free tool for educational social networks. A teacher can set up a virtual classroom in which students are free to share documents and ideas as they choose. In addition to a desktop version, Edmodo also has versions for smartphones and tablets in both the iOS and Android platforms.

The sharing of material is quite a powerful application for social networks. According to an interesting study done by the Pew Internet and American Life project, it was found that photos and videos have become key social currencies online.[2] Their study showed that 46 percent of adult Internet users post original photos or videos online that they themselves have created, and 41 percent of adult Internet users take photos or videos that they have found online and repost them on sites designed for sharing images with many people.

The sites people use for this posting and sharing include Pinterest (http://pinterest.com), Instagram (http://instagram.com/#), and Tumblr (www.tumblr.com), all of which are supported on mobile devices. Their research showed that Pinterest appealed more to women and that the other sites appealed to both genders. Of course, when it comes to sharing images and videos, Flickr (www.flickr.com), Facebook (www.facebook.com), and YouTube(www.youtube.com) have to top the list in terms of noncommercial image and video sites, with YouTube claiming 10 percent of all Internet traffic during peak hours.[3] Although this Pew study focused on adults, their research on young people is just as interesting. This study showed that the typical US teen sent and received a greater number of texts in 2011 than in 2009. Overall, 75 percent of all teens text. The median number of texts sent on a typical day by teens twelve to seventeen rose from fifty in 2009 to sixty in 2011. They found that girls were the most enthusiastic texters, with a median of one hundred texts a day in 2011, compared with fifty for boys the same age. This is a staggering number of messages and, to be honest, I'm not sure I have enough information crossing my plate every day to support this level of texting. Of course, many of these messages between students are of a personal nature, but some could just as easily be about academic work—and it is this application that has some educators wary of the medium.

One teacher told me of a student who was sending text messages to a colleague in the library during an exam. A student there would look up answers and text them back. As I mentioned before, the main problem was that the test was asking questions for which the Internet (or library) was the answer. Yes, the student should not have been doing this, but the blame needs to be shared with those who think a curriculum based on regurgitation of factoids represents real learning.

The aforementioned Pew study found that 63 percent of all teens say they exchange text messages *every day* with people in their lives. This far surpasses the frequency with which they pick other forms of daily communication, including making voice calls by cell phone (39 percent do that with others every day), face-to-face socializing outside of school (35 percent), social network site messaging (29 percent), instant messaging (22 percent), talking on landlines (19 percent), and e-mailing (6 percent).

With the rapid rise in smartphone growth, some carriers (e.g., Verizon) are offering free voice and texting as part of their data plan.[4] In other words, they know where the traffic is heading as our phones continue to look less and less like the mobile phones we were happy with just a few years ago. The smartphone has incorporated an incredible number of technologies into its compact form. It is a camera, a calendar, a video game console, a web browser, a texting tool— and, for some, a telephone. As more features get added to these devices, the role of this single piece of hardware in social learning will only grow.

There is little doubt the Watering Hole has turned into a river that flows through the Internet to reach most teens—and, I would bet, most younger children as well. Interestingly, I came late to the texting party but now use it with some regularity (although at levels far below that of the typical teenager).

THE RISE OF THE COLLABORATORY

There is a challenge that emerges when using social networking tools in the classroom, and that is the tendency for students to form groups only with their good friends. This means that the popular kids will have an easy time forming groups, and the less popular kids may find themselves without any group to join. For this reason, it is important for the teacher to ensure that every student is in a group, and the group may turn out not to be filled with close colleagues but with those assigned there by the teacher to foster the growth of new ideas. The freshness of perspective that comes from outside influences is very important, especially when working on creative projects. One technological tool that helps in this regard is Google+ in which participants form various circles. One circle may be family, another, close friends. You can create a circle of any grouping you wish—including class projects. People in a circle not only share messages and ideas with each other, but they can also go to the "hangout" and have video conferences with the others in their group.

When we think about Watering Hole technologies, it is essential to understand that the teacher's role is to be a collaborator. It is not enough to have students working in groups if the teacher is not collaborating as well. The opportunities for the co-learning model are quite rich. It is common for teachers in these environments to gain new insights into a subject area as a result of ideas coming from the students. In this sense, the classroom becomes a "collaborator," where everyone is at the Watering Hole together.

One reason technology brings so much to the Watering Hole is its ability to transcend space and time. Face-to-face learning requires that everyone be in the same place at the same time. Online social learning tools, however, include support for asynchronous interactions from anywhere in the world. Tools such as Google+ support both synchronous and asynchronous communication, making them quite valuable in an educational setting. In my own experience teaching courses at Walden University, most of our interaction is asynchronous. This allows me to have students in Kenya, the United States, and elsewhere, with me commuting back and forth between Brazil and the United States and never having to think about time zones. When students want face time with me, we schedule video chats through tools like Skype or through a hangout at Google+. One of the benefits of having classes with students from all over the world is the richness of ideas that such diversity encourages. This kind of diversity is not possible in the physical classroom where all students are present at the same time.

THE RISE OF BLOGS AND WIKIS

When the World Wide Web was first developed, people had tools with which they could create their own web pages. Most websites were one-way streets where the flow of information was directed to a largely anonymous audience. These kinds of sites still have a lot of value as informational resources, but over the years other types of web-based tools became available. Blogs (short for weblogs) are sites with a single main author (like a traditional website) but with the added ability for others to post comments related to various post-ings for others to see. In general such postings are moderated by the site author to keep the comments relevant, but the ethos of a good blogger is to support diverse points of view.

One of my favorite blogs is the Instructables site (www .instructables.com). This site is a place where people are free to add instructions on how to build just about anything—a self-directed automatic lawn mower, a rocket built only with materials from an office supply store—you name it, they are likely to have it! And, if someone hasn't posted plans for a project you are working on, you are free to add your own project to the mix. But, in addition to being a place where you can find and post instructions for various projects, you can also comment on the postings of others. These commentaries are often quite helpful—for example, providing alternate sources for otherwise hard-to-find parts for a specific gadget.

From a personal perspective, I do a lot of my sharing of ideas through my blog, not through one of my websites. I don't do this just because it is easier, but because it allows outside commentaries on my ideas that I find quite useful. This was a big transition for me. I used to write periodic "white papers" that were posted on my website, but these were one-way communication tools—more like broadcast television in which conversations with viewers is impossible. In my case, communication was encouraged through e-mail, but the blog makes this whole process far easier and more transparent.

Blogs are great Watering Hole places, but, for the really brave, there is another kind of tool called the *wiki*. Wikis are like blogs in that they accept postings and comments but with the important difference that the content of the original posting can be modified by others. You might think that this would lead to chaos, but there are some compelling examples of wikis that grow in value for the simple reason that the people who use them have a vested interest in keeping them accurate and current.

The most famous of these is *Wikipedia* (www.wikipedia.org)—an informational resource that has grown in popularity to the point that most traditional online encyclopedias have ceased to exist. In the past, online encyclopedias included offerings from Microsoft (*Encarta*) and the famed *Encyclopaedia Britannica*—only the latter of these remaining in business. Because *Wikipedia* is maintained by volunteer editors, it is logical to ask if the entries are any good. Overall, the quality of articles is excellent, largely because they are written by the very people who want to use the resource. The downside is that articles of little interest to the volunteers just don't get the treatment they might deserve.

It is interesting to note the continuing resistance to *Wikipedia* by many schools—probably because of the volunteer status of the contributors. But, based on that argument, one should not use the *Oxford English Dictionary (OED)* either. This dictionary, considered the most accurate English dictionary in the world, had a very *Wikipedia*-like start. In *The Professor and the Madman: A Tale of Murder, Insanity, and the Making of the* Oxford English Dictionary, Simon Winchester talks about the volunteer readers used in compiling this amazing book—some of whom were in hospitals for the criminally insane.[5] Yes, the *OED* has professional editors, but without the help of a huge cadre of volunteers this amazing effort might never have come to fruition.

I use *Wikipedia* for academic topics all the time, and find it to be quite accurate. I also look at postings on topics in which I have some expertise to see if the entries need to be edited. We tend to take care of the tools we wish to rely on, and for many people, *Wikipedia* is such a tool. Far from being a mere Watering Hole, *Wikipedia* is a virtual ocean of collaboration, even if the collaborators never communicate directly with each other. This all works because of a few simple rules that can be applied to other wikis as well. The Wikimedia Foundation rules apply to all entries:[6]

- A neutral point of view is the most important rule in changing pages.
- Anyone can change articles without making a username.
- The "wiki process" is the way to decide what is put on the project.
- All writing is freely available to everyone.

In my teaching at Walden University we make steady use of online discussions and blogs. Because our doctoral courses are based on inquiry-centric models that have culminating projects, constant student engagement is essential and a critical part of this is their engagement with each other. I suggest a discussion topic, for example, and for the next two weeks (in addition to other course-related work) students engage in discussions around this topic and respond to postings by other students. These postings help clarify thinking, and often reveal ideas that none of us would have had on our own. Blog entries by the students are a bit nicer because they allow more media to be incorporated than a usual text chat. And, because these blogs (unlike the class discussions) are in a public space, there is nothing to keep outsiders from joining the conversation!

PEDAGOGICAL THOUGHTS AROUND THE TECHNOLOGICAL WATERING HOLE

Howard Rheingold spends a lot of time thinking about truly collaborative learning—a process he calls *peeragogy*. The idea behind this model comes from his observation that

> with YouTube, Wikipedia, search engines, free chatrooms, blogs, wikis, and video communication, today's self-learners have power never dreamed of before. What does any group of self-learners need to know in order to self-organize learning about any topic? . . .
>
> This project seeks to empower the worldwide population of self-motivated learners who use digital media to connect with each other, to co-construct knowledge of how to co-learn. Co-learning is ancient; the capacity for learning by imitation and more, to teach others what we know, is the essence of human culture. We are human because we learn together. Today, however, the advent of digital production media and distribution/communication networks has raised the power of co-learning to a new level.[7]

The idea of "we are human because we learn together" is a thread that has run through pedagogical thought at least since the time of Lev Vygotsky's pioneering work on social constructivism. And work in this area continues today.

For example, Paulo Blikstein wrote a paper on his interpretations of the work of the famous Brazilian educator, Paulo Friere. (Friere's work was, in turn, influenced by the social constructivist models of Lev Vygotsky.) As Blikstein says of his own experiences with students,

> A learner-centered, culturally aware Freirean aesthetic raises the question of how to manage a classroom in which every student has a different background, as well as diverse interests and talents. Ostensibly, this would entail a significant amount of extra work from the teacher. Our data suggest that such a diversity-sensitive approach may in fact help alleviate the teachers' burden and improve their relationship with students.

> ... I have shown that, following an initially laborious and intensive contact with students, through which I became familiar with student ideas, ways of working, passions, and talents, subsequent interactions became much easier. Not only did students become more autonomous and responsible, they learned to teach one another. By allowing students to work on their own ideas, not only could I more effectively understand their epistemology, but unprecedented motivation and engagement were generated. This kind of environment also enables teachers to spend less time as discipline-enforcers.

> ... The observations (also) suggest that the lack of strict rules did not generate an "anything goes" or unchallenging environment, in which students would have engaged in activities that are only playful or amusing. In Heliópolis and other workshop [locations], on the contrary, teachers reported being impressed by the number of hours students invested and by students' serious attitude toward the work. In turn, students reported that they were driven by teachers' "fair play" and genuine respect.[8]

Although Blikstein's work was conducted in a classroom, his observations apply equally well when the constraints of time and space are removed. True collaboration is powerful indeed, and, as we have seen, technology has some strong roles to play in the facilitation of Watering Hole activities. Of course, not all Watering Hole technologies are Internet-based.

OFFLINE WATERING HOLES

One fine example of technology-based Watering Holes that don't use the Internet comes through the research at the University of Durham by Professor Liz Burd and her colleagues.[9] Burd's concern was that too often classroom-based educational technology requires pupils to adopt a "move-to-use" approach that can detract from technology's educational value. In other words, when a student wants to engage with another group she has to physically go from one place to another in a traditional setting. The outcome of the Durham research is a proposal for a new learning environment called *SynergyNet*. This learning environment is technology rich, where touch-screen computers are seamlessly integrated into the fabric of a classroom without intruding on the main focus of the activity. This approach facilitated classroom dialogue and pupil collaboration.

Central to SynergyNet is a new form of desk that contains a large built-in multitouch surface. Unlike traditional interactive whiteboards, multitouch surfaces can detect simultaneous contacts by fingers or pens. Therefore, two or more pupils can operate the desk at the same time. So, feasibly, a single multitouch desk can operate as a set of individual computerized work spaces or a single large digital workspace allowing pupils to work individually and to cooperate on a task. If a student wants to share information with kids at another table, rapidly dragging the documents off the table in the direction of the other one causes the file to move to the new location.

The idea that a piece of technology-enhanced furniture can improve collaboration skills is quite exciting, especially given that multitouch LCD flat screens are becoming affordable.

There are many ways non-Internet-based technology can enhance Watering Hole activities, and the task is to open ourselves to using them whenever possible. For example, students can create templates for making multimedia projects, and then share these with their colleagues over the school network—or even through removable flash drives. A student who has a great collection of sharable images can make these available to colleagues in the same way. Students with good sound editing skills can be the volunteer sound editors for other student projects using recorded audio. This method of learning by "wandering around" has some similarities to the sorts of activities used in architectural studios, where projects get looked at with a fresh view by other architects not working on that particular design.

Now we move to the Cave to explore what technology use in this environment looks like and how it might grow in the future.

CHAPTER 9

Technological Caves

In the 1950s my mind was wandering in the direction of science and technology. A lot of this had to do with *Sputnik*—the launch of which captured my mind along with those of others who watched the October sky for a glimpse of the world's first "artificial moon." My parents encouraged my interests, and one day a large package arrived for me. This box contained all the parts needed to create the Geniac, my first digital "computer." In fact, the kit was not to build a real computer—it had no relays or vacuum tubes—only pressboard circles and a base in which electrical contacts could be placed, along with a row of lights and a single flashlight battery.

Because the Geniac was not a real computer, what could you do with it? The answer is that you could use it to build a lot of neat computational tools for playing games like Nim (a mathematical game of strategy). Instead of relays and tubes, it used human power to move the connection wheels from one location to another. You would hook up wires to the various contacts (screws, as I recall). These wires defined the "program" you would run. As I moved the wheels, different lights would turn on or off, giving me the data needed to determine how the wheels should be turned next. Even though the concept was quite simple, the Geniac could be used for some great projects and involved a lot of reflective thought to use! I spent countless hours playing with this crude machine, and probably developed some good thinking strategies as a result. I was in my Cave!

COGNITIVE CAVES

If the Watering Hole is home to Vygotsky's social constructivism, then the Cave is where we find Piaget's cognitive constructivism to be at the forefront. In the history of educational technology, the name associated with bringing modern technology–supported constructivist principles into play is that of MIT's Seymour Papert.

Papert worked with Jean Piaget at the University of Geneva from 1958 to 1963 and is widely considered the most brilliant and successful of Piaget's protégés.[1] Piaget once said that "no one understands my ideas as well as Papert." Papert devoted his life to thinking about how schools should work based on these theories of learning.

For example, he used Piaget's work in his development of the Logo programming language while at MIT. The language itself was created in 1967 by Danny Bobrow, Wally Feurzeig, and Cynthia Solomon under Papert's guidance.[2] Personal computers were not in existence at the time, and graphic displays were in their infancy, so the original versions of Logo ran on large minicomputers.

The core idea behind Logo was for it to be a tool to improve the way children think and solve problems. In the beginning, a small robot called the *turtle* was developed. This device was controlled by computer programs written in Logo by the children themselves, and children used it to solve problems. For example, if a child wanted the turtle to move on a triangular path, then she might write: *Repeat 3 [Forward 10 Right 120]*, which would have the turtle move ten steps, then turn 120 degrees to the right, and repeat this motion three times. As computers with graphic displays were developed, the turtle appeared as an icon on the screen where images were drawn. The interface to physical turtles was still supported in many cases, but today most Logo users rely purely on screen-drawn images.

Papert insisted that a simple programming language that children could learn—such as Logo—can also have advanced functionality for expert users. Papert refers to this characteristic of Logo as "no floor, no ceiling." Because Logo was based on the artificial intelligence (AI) programming language, Lisp, the richness of Logo was guaranteed.

The motivation behind using this language was not to develop programming skills per se, but for students, through the creation of their own programs, to develop problem-solving skills that could be applied in other areas. In this sense, Logo programming was both a creative and reflective discipline, hence, its inclusion in this chapter.

LOGO TODAY

There are a wide variety of Logo versions available today, ranging from simple standard Logos such as Softronix's MSWLogo (www .softronix.com) to extremely rich versions such as NetLogo (http:// ccl.northwestern.edu/netlogo), designed to be used for, among other things, the study of emergent behavior in complex systems (how birds flock, for example). Both of these versions are free, and they are but two of the many versions available.

As for the kinds of things kids can do, one project is to write a program that draws a square on the screen. That can be done by writing a simple procedure:

```
to square:size
repeat 4 [forward:size right 90]
end
```

The ":size" in this procedure represents the value of a variable we have called "size." So, in order to draw a square 300 units on a side, we would simply type "square 300" and the figure would be drawn on the screen.

In Logo, a square is made by turning 90 degrees at each corner, meaning that to get back to the starting position, the turtle turns 360 degrees. In experimenting with Logo, students find that all polygons are built by a total number of turns equal to 360 or multiples thereof. Our hypothetical student may want to experiment with his square and

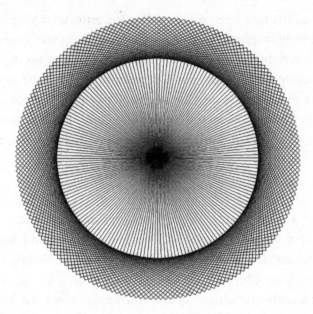

Figure 9.1

use it to make more complex shapes. For example, the following procedure draws a nice picture on the screen:

```
to pattern:size
repeat 180 [square:size right 2]
end
```

Note that the pattern is made by drawing a square, turning two
degrees, and then repeating this process 180 times. Figure 9.1 shows
what happens if we type "pattern 300."

The only drawback of Logo is the requirement that commands be
typed—a skill that may exceed the capabilities of young children.
Recent developments in programming languages have solved this
problem. The Scratch language (http://scratch.mit.edu), developed at
the MIT Media Lab, is a perfect example of this new kind of Logoish
language. With Scratch, programs are created by assembling pieces

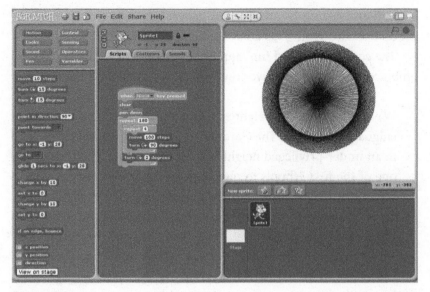

Figure 9.2

together to produce the desired results—somewhat like assembling a jigsaw puzzle, but a puzzle with an infinite number of possibilities. For example, the complex pattern we just created would be created in Scratch as shown in figure 9.2.

Although Scratch does not yet support the creation of procedures, this will change in the future, making the programs even easier to create. One feature of Scratch is that the user can choose from a wide number of natural languages to label the pieces. This is of great help in the multilingual classroom where English may not be the dominant language.

WHAT'S THE POINT?

The idea that programming is both a creative and reflective discipline is of great value when a student writes a program that doesn't work as expected. It is through the process of fixing a program that tremendous learning takes place. Furthermore, this learning can be applied to problem solving in other areas. Papert has long championed the process of "debugging" as a key element of learning.

The concept of "hard fun" applies to the kind of activities children embrace when they start working with Logo. As Papert has said,

> Way back in the mid-eighties a first grader gave me a nugget of language that helps. The Gardner Academy (an elementary school in an under-privileged neighborhood of San Jose, California) was one of the first schools to own enough computers for students to spend significant time with them every day. Their introduction, for all grades, was learning to program, in the computer language Logo, at an appropriate level. A teacher heard one child using these words to describe the computer work: "It's fun. It's hard. It's Logo." I have no doubt that this kid called the work fun *because* it was hard rather than *in spite* of being hard.

> Once I was alerted to the concept of "hard fun" I began listening for it and heard it over and over. It is expressed in many different ways, all of which all boil down to the conclusion that everyone likes hard challenging things to do. But they have to be the right things matched to the individual and to the culture of the times.[3]

HARD FUN IN ACTION

If you want to have some hard fun on your own, try writing a Logo program that draws the picture shown in figure 9.3.

Believe it or not, this complex figure was created with one simple procedure:

```
to star:size:limit
if:size <:limit [stop]
repeat 5 [fd:size rt 144 star:size/2:limit]
end
```

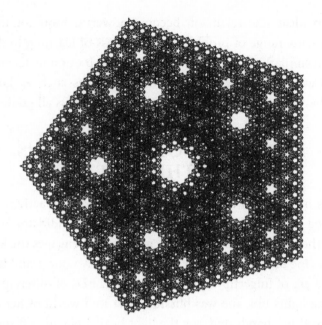

Figure 9.3

Over the years, I've seen numerous children master the intricacies of Logo to create amazingly complex projects that they understand on a deep level. The challenge we face as educators is creating a climate in which these kinds of rich geometric investigations are not only allowed, but they are also commonplace.

Because Logo is a list processing language, it is in no way restricted to the creation of graphic images. For example, the procedure to create figure 9.3 uses recursion in that it is defined in terms that include itself (the procedure "recurs" in its own definition). This seemingly strange concept is known to most children through nursery tales such as *The House That Jack Built* or Christmas carols such as *The Twelve Days of Christmas*. Children can create programs that work with words and other objects that they encounter in daily life. My emphasis on graphics reflects a personal interest, not, in any way, the limitations of Logo.

Deep ideas like recursion become powerful tools for thinking about a wide range of problems. The process of learning to debug a program similarly develops transferable skills. If our only technology-based Cave tools were programming languages such as Logo, we would have enough richness to last a lifetime across all grade levels.

EXPLORING OTHER REGIONS OF THE CAVE

There is no question that the kinds of programming activities we've described stimulate reflection and are thus good candidates for inclusion in the digital Cave. In fact, any activity that engages the learner's mind is ripe for inclusion. For example, we gave our granddaughter Bianca a set of fingertip rings with built-in LEDs of different colors. With the lights out, she was blissfully lost in a world of her own as she moved her hands and saw the light beams playing off the walls. Next, I ran a program called Glow Doodle (http://scripts.mit.edu /~eric_r/glowdoodle) created by Eric Rosenbaum and Jay Silver at the MIT Media Lab. This software allowed her to paint on the computer screen using her LED-lit hand gestures that were tracked by the built-in web camera. Activities of this sort can stimulate lots of what-if? thinking in children of any age. For example, what kinds of images can be created with this technology-enhanced finger-painting program? What motor skills do activities like this promote? The list goes on.

For older students, mathematical construction programs such as GeoGebra (www.geogebra.org) can engage students for hours of reflective thought as they construct algebraic and geometric representations of core mathematical ideas. For example, the pizza-cutting problem mentioned in chapter 2 lends itself to rich exploration with tools like this. Anyone addicted to the television series *Numb3rs* (now in reruns) can explore lots of the ideas explored in that show using GeoGebra.

But sooner or later it is time to emerge from the Cave and move to the world of application in the space of Life.

CHAPTER 10

Technological Life Spaces

Some of the technologies from the previous chapter also have relevance in the domain of the Life learning space. The critical idea here is that students create artifacts they can share with others. This moves us from constructivism to constructionism.

For many years, Seymour Papert focused on the Piagetian cognitive constructivist aspect of Logo in which the critical element was the kind of internal thought processes and models that were being developed by the learner. However, because the end result of a student Logo project is a finished artifact—a program that can be shared with others, the existence of this artifact also puts Logo into the Life domain.

It can be argued that it is only through the actual building of something that we can be said to really know and understand it. Because education is so focused on our heads, and not in developing the application side of things, we have students graduating with a lot of information they think they know but may not truly understand.

One amazing example of the kinds of misunderstandings that permeate our lives was found a long time ago when researchers at Harvard University interviewed college graduates (on graduation day) and had them explain why it is warmer in the summer and colder in the winter.[1] The researchers found that most of the people they interviewed thought it was warmer in the summer because "the earth is closer to the sun." Not only was this misperception locked in the minds of the students, it was present in faculty members as well. Even students who had taken lots of courses in physics held on to their incorrect ideas. The research then moved to high schools where students and teachers alike held similar misperceptions, even though they were taught that the seasons are caused by the tilt of the earth on its axis as it moves in its nearly circular orbit around the sun. (Contrary to the pictures in many science books, the orbits of most planets are nearly perfect circles.)

Why does this misperception exist, even when we teach the real reason to students? Probably because their life experiences were such that they noticed a strong relationship between distance and heat. When children put their hands too close to a stove burner, for example, they feel a lot of heat, and this helps build (through experience) the idea that temperature is related to the distance from the hot object. These childhood experiences are so strong that no amount of purely head-based learning seems to overcome them. And the problem is not limited to explaining the seasons. It applies as well to their ideas about the phases of the moon (caused, according to many students, from the shadow cast by the earth).

Several years ago I conducted an experiment of my own. I was leading a workshop for middle and high school science teachers and I presented the following challenge: "Imagine you are standing on the moon and you release a pencil from your hand. What will happen? Will it fall to the lunar surface, stay in place, or be attracted back to the earth?" Only a few teachers correctly said that the pencil would fall to the lunar surface. The others were split on the idea it would either hover in space (balanced by the earth's gravitational attraction) or would return to earth "because if the pull of the earth is strong enough to hold the moon in place, it would suck something as light as a pencil back to earth pretty fast."

Now these were bright people who had misperceptions based on their mental models of gravitational forces. For example, we often talk about gravity attracting objects to earth (Newton's apple, for example).

But rarely do we talk about the correct observation that the apple is also pulling the earth toward *it*. Because the mass of the objects we drop is so small, we assume that the force just works one way.

So how do we go about fixing these kinds of misconceptions? Lectures don't work, and for the most part neither do conversations and personal reflections. Campfires, Watering Holes, and Caves are not enough. It is only through the things we explore in the Life domain that many challenges can be addressed.

For example, can you design a working mechanical model that illustrates why the earth has seasons? What materials would you need? How would it operate? This could be a great project for you and your students to pursue.

Sometimes the teacher's job should just be to nudge students in the right direction when they are exploring things in the domain of Life. I once had a fifth-grade student in a robotics workshop who was trying to support a structure with straight legs made from soda straws. The weight of the structure was so great that the straws collapsed. I asked her to take a soda straw and bend it into a rectangular shape and to see what happened when she pressed on opposite corners. The shape was quite flexible. I then had her repeat the process with a straw bent into a triangular shape, and she quickly found that triangles are stable structures—they hold their shape under force. As the light bulb went on in her head, she commented that she saw many triangular structures every day—bridge trusses, and so on, and now understood why triangular shapes are so commonplace. She also told me that, on reflection, a teacher in a math class had told her that triangles were stable, but that she forgot about it. This may be because she never experienced this property on her own. She went to work building triangular legs for her robot, and it worked perfectly (see figure 10.1).

Theoretical knowledge was enhanced by actual physical application of the ideas. This also addresses another important concept—the transference of knowledge across disciplines. This transference needs to be something the teacher watches out for. Basically, I ask myself

Figure 10.1

what that child already knows from another subject that has applicability here. The transference of skills is so important that it represents one-third of the Next Generation Science Standards. The key to success in this area is practice—especially if your teaching is in a specific content area.

Let me give an example. There is a famous mathematics problem called the Seven Bridges of Königsberg—a problem that led to the creation of graph theory in the mid-18th century. Basically, this problem describes a pair of islands connected to the mainland by several bridges and asks if there exists a path by which one could cross each bridge only once and return to where he started. (It turns out, in that case, the answer was "no.") One of my mathematician friends was sharing this problem with his class, and I pointed out that in our local city of Recife, Brazil, one could find an island that would be perfect for the students to explore (see figure 10.2).

Rather than deal with an old Prussian city, students could apply their knowledge of local geography to the exploration of this math

Figure 10.2

problem. This helped engage students in a problem that was no longer abstract but quite concrete.

Of course, another method might be to explore the original problem and then ask the students to find other cities with islands and see if the bridges there could be crossed once, ultimately leading back to the starting point. The key element of transference is being aware of opportunities to explore it, even if this means exploring topics that might not be usually thought of as connected. To get you started, here are a few topics for which connections might exist—but the important thing is finding them on your own.

What connects

- Renaissance art to mathematics?
- Galaxies to hurricanes?
- Electric cars to history?
- Physiology to mathematics?

HANDS-ON MEANS UP TO THE ARMPITS

The importance of hands-on learning was made with great frequency by Sally Osberg, the founding executive director of the Children's Discovery Museum (CDM) in San Jose, California. This huge (fifty-two-thousand-square-foot) purple building is home to a resource of great value to the community. It is a place where kids can experiment with a wide variety of objects and make concrete observations about the world in which they live. My concern is that for too many children, children's museums like the CDM are about the only places they get to actually build things and have other constructionist experiences. Their schools are so devoted to head-based learning that there are few if any resources widely available for students to use.

There are many ways to bring constructionist tools and methods into schools. Some great ideas, applicable in schools, come from the MIT Media Lab—an acknowledged leader in developing technologies for hands-on learning. Through the Lifelong Kindergarten group, Mitch Resnick oversees a tremendous range of creative efforts devoted to children. For example, Jay Silver and Eric Rosenbaum, the creators of Glow Doodle, mentioned in chapter 9, have worked on many tools and invention kits appropriate for young people (and those of any age willing to try new things out).

One of their latest inventions is the MaKey MaKey (www .makeymakey.com) (see figure 10.3).

This inexpensive device consists of a circuit board connected to your computer through a standard USB port that allows almost anything to be turned into a keyboard. For example, using any keyboard-based musical instrument software, students can choose to play notes by touching bananas. Or they can wire the steps of a staircase so that as people go up and down they can play music. One of their other products, Drawdio (http://web.media.mit.edu/~silver /drawdio), allows people to draw lines on paper with a soft pencil, and then, by touching the line in different places, play musical tones. The frequency of the tone is based on the electrical resistance of the

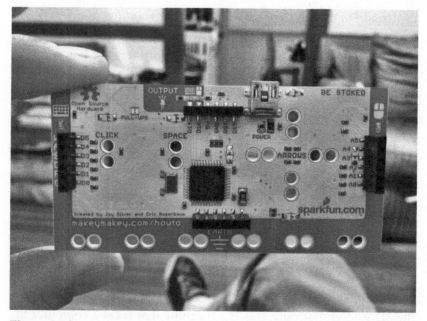

Figure 10.3
Source: MaKey MaKey.

graphite line, with longer lines producing lower tones than shorter ones. Any resistive medium can be used to make music. For example, a stream of water from a faucet can be used to make a theremin-like instrument, where different notes can be played based on where the player's hand interrupts the water stream.

A simple tool such as Drawdio can be used to help students understand the concept of electrical resistance, not because they studied Ohm's law but because of direct physical experience. Of course, once the experience happens, it is the perfect time to introduce some fundamental principles (such as Ohm's law) that would likely be quickly forgotten if presented without the involvement on a physical level.

Make: magazine (http://blog.makezine.com/home-page-include) is a tremendous resource for those interested in bringing more of the Life space into education. *Make:*'s founder, Dale Dougherty, created the motto, "If you can't hack it, you don't own it." The idea is that true ownership of a gadget comes with the understanding that you might take it apart and repurpose it in neat ways. Of course, many of the projects in *Make:* involve building things from scratch. For example, projects range from extracting your own DNA using chemicals found in the kitchen, to building a head-mounted water cannon. Their website contains not only article and blogs but also instructional videos on how to build things. All that is left is for the teacher to take some of these activities and bring them into the curriculum. Ideally, schools should have the makerspaces we talked about in chapter 5, where students can tinker, build, and work on construction projects that might take several weeks.

RISE OF THE DESKTOP FABRICATOR

One technology that is starting to make an appearance in schools is the 3D printer. Basically, this is a machine that takes a computer file describing a three-dimensional object and then builds the actual part out of (for example) plastic. Initially developed as rapid prototyping systems for industry, these machines can be quite expensive. But systems perfect for educational use are now available at very reasonable prices. With these tools, kids can build just about anything they want. If they can draw it, the system can build it. Best of all, some of the less expensive 3D printers are quite small and fit well in a usual classroom, as seen in the picture of the Cubify printer in figure 10.4.

There are several choices for inexpensive (under $2,000) fabricators. These range from the MakerBot to the fabricator made by Cubify. The MakerBot was one of the first fabricator kits. It is a bit tricky to set up, but the process of building it can be a great student project. Cubify, however, is ready to use right out of the box and has a wide variety of templates students can modify to make objects such as bracelets as well as 3D modeling software that can be used to make anything you wish within the size constraints (roughly six inches on a side). Cornell University has developed its own inexpensive fabricator (www.fabathome.org) that is interesting because it supports the

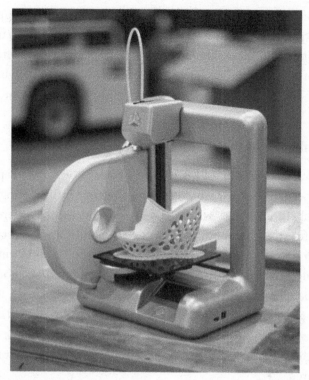

Figure 10.4
Source: Courtesy 3D Systems.

use of different materials. You can build with plastic or even with food such as chocolate and Cheez Whiz (although you are not likely to use these last two materials in combination with each other)!

3D Design Tools

The spectrum of freely available design tools is quite amazing. Autodesk, best known for their high-end computer-assisted design (CAD) software, has released a series of free programs, Autodesk 123D apps (www.123dapp.com) for the design of parts that can then be built on your own fabricator or using an outside service. One of the more popular 3D design tools is SketchUp (www.sketchup.com). The free version of this program can be modified to export your designs in the format expected by desktop fabricators, and it is fairly easy to use. That said, designing in three dimensions is a skill that is not mastered overnight. Fortunately, people with fabricators are happy to do whatever it takes to have the computer craft objects of their own creation.

The Challenge of the Blank Screen

Many years ago, in one of his lectures, I heard Seymour Papert talk about those children for whom a blank screen is intimidating. Rather than jump in and start writing Logo procedures, they were frozen with the fear they had nothing to write. His solution was to start these kids with existing procedures they could edit to do different things. For example, a procedure that draws a square could be modified to draw a pentagon, or it could be used by new procedures to create complex geometric patterns. Once students became comfortable with editing preexisting procedures, they were ready to embark on software of their own design. The blank screen was no longer something to be feared.

If a blank programming screen can be intimidating, imagine how some people might react to being thrown into the pool of 3D design software with which they are expected to design something to be built on a desktop fabricator. Aside from the fact that the curriculum rarely focuses on 3D geometries, the prospect of designing all but the simplest shapes in any 3D program takes a lot of effort. There are lots of things to think about—the design of the shape itself and the orientation of the shape to allow it to be built easily in the fabricator.

Fortunately, help is at hand. For example, Thingiverse (www .thingiverse.com) is a website on which people can post 3D designs to share with others. These designs can be downloaded and modified by anyone, because they are placed in the public domain. For example, because of my interest in robotics, I need to be able to step down the speed of ordinary DC motors with gears. Gears, it turns out, are tricky to design. Fortunately, Thingiverse has a large collection of gear designs in its library that anyone can download and modify to meet specific needs before sending them to a desktop replicator. Once I've designed a part, I can upload the design to Thingiverse to be shared with others, and this increases the value of the collection even more!

Making Things without a Fabricator

Suppose you want to make something and you don't have a fabricator at school? The 100kGarages (www.100kgarages.com) project links designers to places where designs can be made and then shipped to you a few days later. This project is a perfect example of how the maker movement is growing. This topic is the core of the book *Makers: The New Industrial Revolution,* by Chris Anderson.[2] He makes a point in his book that crafting things by hand was once more common than it is today—although it is making a comeback, in part thanks to these inexpensive technologies that can turn visions into parts!

THE MAKER'S CULTURE

Recent generations seem to have adopted a screen-based culture as kids spend countless hours in front of their computers and only use their hands to type and move a mouse. Although there can be wonderful things done in that world (as we've explored in earlier chapters), there is also a need to learn to think with our hands, not just our heads.

I was fortunate enough to grow up in a maker culture. My dad had a shop in the basement and made everything from coffee tables to clocks—clocks made with gears he cut himself. My exposure was not as a bystander, but as someone who, in helping him, was also bitten by the fabrication bug. In my case, the topic of interest was electronics and I would scour the neighborhood alleys looking for old radios that were being discarded so I could dismantle them for parts. By the time I was in high school, I had an amateur radio license and was able to converse with people all over the world using equipment I had built myself, from scratch. I still have, and use, a multimeter I bought back in the 1950s to help me troubleshoot my projects.

THE FABBER'S ETHOS

Although it doesn't get talked about much, the fabber's ethos is important—and I got mine through my dad. One day I was helping him finish a chest of drawers, and he was sanding the undersides of the drawers—areas that would never be seen. I asked him why he was putting attention to parts no one would ever see. "No one will ever know if you did that," I said. His response was priceless: "I will."

Once we get fabbing tools in the hands of kids, they end up learning far more than the mechanics of building things. They learn the elements of good design—perhaps moving to the realm of elegance. These skills will last a lifetime, even if our kids never build anything again.

The point here is not just the ability to design and build complex parts, but to trigger inventive ideas than can lead to entrepreneurship. This topic is especially important if we want to grow sources of good-paying jobs. The days when the huge companies (General Motors, General Mills, General Electric, and their brethren) controlled the pace of innovation has passed. This is a recent phenomenon driven, in part, by the rise of personal fabrication tools and software.

I remember when I helped start Koala Technologies (manufacturer of the first touch-sensitive graphics tablet for personal computers). Huge outside investments were needed to pay for the tooling needed to build these devices. Such was the cost of life in the world of atoms. Software developers had it easy by comparison. Armed with little more than a computer, a credit card, and a great idea, software developers could bypass the venture capitalists and start businesses from home. Now, this freedom (and power) has come to entrepreneurship in manufacturing. Whether it is one part or a million, the investments needed to set up shop are quite modest. Once the business has grown to the right size, you can invest in the tools of mass production. Until then, fabrication on demand works pretty well.

Why is this aspect of the Life space important in education? The simple answer is that we have entered a new world when it comes to growing the economy. The dot-com world has morphed into the world of fabrication, and our students need to be as comfortable working with the new tools as previous generations were with the old ones.

Of course, there are those who will argue that there is no place in the curriculum for actually building anything. That is not true. The process of creating a design to be fabbed provides practical application of ideas explored in mathematics, physics, and other subjects.

OTHER FABRICATION OPTIONS

What if your school simply lacks the space and resources to build your own fabrication lab? The Hackerspace project (http://hackerspaces.org /wiki) may be able to help. This resource maintains a list of hacker-spaces all over the world where people (including kids) who want to design and build stuff can do so. They even issue a "hackerspace passport" for those who visit multiple spaces to get stamped as they enter!

An inexpensive option for getting started is to use a computer-controlled paper cutter like the one from Silhouette (www .silhouetteamerica.com), which cuts everything from paper and card-board to thin vinyl sheets. Once objects are cut, they can be folded into the final shape for your project. Say you want to build a polyhe-dron. You could create the polygons for the faces that are connected on a flat sheet of paper so that when they are cut out, they can be folded neatly into the final shape. Simple gears can be made by cutting thin sheets of cardboard into the gear's shape, and then gluing mul-tiple layers of your cutouts together to give the structure some strength. For a very small investment, paper cutters like the Silhouette are a great way to get started with fabrication at almost any grade level. Combine a computer-controlled cutter with a color printer, and students can make really nice-looking gadgets in a short period of time.

If your goal is to make flat objects with complex contours, paper and thin cardboard may not be robust enough. This is where CNC (computer numerical control) machines come in handy. Big versions of these systems are commonplace in modern shops and factories. And, similar to 3D fabricators, desktop versions exist as well, such as those from MiDIYCNC (www.mydiycnc.com) and Inventables (www.inventables.com). One nice thing about these fabricators is that because they work with flat objects, the designs can be created with two-dimensional graphics software—a format with which many people are already familiar. As for the software itself, the graphics packages most people use are specifically designed for CNC, and a quick search will uncover a tremendous number of good programs, many of which are free. But specialized software may not be needed! Inkscape (http://inkscape.org) is a graphics tool I've grown to love over the years, and it allows finished drawings to be exported as "dxf" files—the kind used to operate simple CNC machines. With this software, if you can draw it, your CNC device can make it.

Once the part you want to build has been designed, you just mount a sheet of plastic or plywood (for example) into the CNC machine and start the program. Similar to 3D replicators, you get to watch the parts as they are being made.

One important difference between the CNC machines and the 3D replicators we've been talking about is that the CNC machines are subtractive—they cut specific parts out of a piece of material. This process produces dust that must be cleaned up, making CNC machines better suited for use in special rooms and not on a table in a classroom, unless a broom and dustpan are readily available. 3D fabricators, however, are additive—building parts by the addition of layers of plastic until the part is finished. There is no scrap or dust to clean up. You build it, remove it from the fabricator, and use it. No muss, no fuss.

ROBOTS COME TO SCHOOL

Of course, building things goes way beyond the use of 3D fabricators and CNC machines. One area of great interest to children is the construction of their own computer-controlled robotic devices. LEGO MINDSTORMS (http://mindstorms.lego.com) was created with this in mind, and it has reflected the constructionist principles of Seymour Papert from the start.

The problem with LEGO-based robotics programs is that the blocks are too expensive for students to keep their own models, so after building and demonstrating a really cool construction, it needs to be taken apart so the materials are available for other kids. This is where building robotics from a combination of recycled materials and parts you make yourself comes in very handy.

My wife is a pioneer in the use of recycled materials in robotics. The advantages are many. First, there is little to no materials cost. Second, students get to use their creativity in building parts for their construction. For example, a flexible hinge might be made with a strip of plastic cut from a soda bottle. One student needed to "raise the level of water behind a dam," and built the "water" out of scrap materials painted blue. This water was raised by a computer-controlled motor that used the screw mechanism from an empty deodorant container.

But the real benefit of building things from recycled materials is that, except for any expensive motors they might contain, they can be taken home afterward. The value of sharing physical artifacts with friends and family cannot be overstated. When our younger daughter, Luciana, was getting her BA in culinary arts, she took a dessert class in which she was asked to build a small replica of a grand piano completely out of chocolate. Her candy sculpture still sits on a display shelf in our home, even though she graduated from college years ago.

Of course, the physical construction of a robot will, at some point, require its connection to motors, lights, and sensors of various kinds, all of which can be controlled by a computer. The most popular interface that does this job is the Arduino card—a small interface board that connects to a computer through a USB port, and provides connections to motors, lights, and sensors. The spectrum of projects done with this card staggers the mind.

Arduino

Arduino (www.arduino.cc) was the brainchild of Massimo Banzi and David Cuartielles in Ivrea, Italy. Their idea was to make a device for controlling student-built interactive designs with less expense than with other prototyping systems available at the time. This vision resulted in a piece of open source hardware that would allow anyone to build a controller for just about anything imaginable. Arduino uses a popular microcontroller chip; and over three hundred thousand of these boards are in the hands of artists, designers, hobbyists, and anyone interested in creating interactive objects or environments.

The Arduino board has multiple digital and analog connections—both inputs and outputs—so you can control motors and other devices, and sense input from things as simple as a switch or a photocell. Because the hardware is open source, you can build one by hand or buy one preassembled for about thirty dollars. I've gone both routes. The process of construction is (for me, anyway) quite enjoyable in itself, but it takes some good soldering skills and the ability to work with very small electronic components.

Programming the Arduino can be done with free software. For example, there is a version of Scratch (Scratch for Arduino (http://seaside.citilab.eu/scratch/arduino) we use in our workshops with educators because it is easy for their students to master. This software can be downloaded for free, but you are in no way limited to creating programs with one tool. The native programming language for Arduino looks a lot like C++ and you can download the compiler for your Arduino board (also free).

A quick web search will show you myriad projects built using this inexpensive interface. Because the Arduino works with all kinds of motors (including servo motors) and all kinds of sensors (temperature, pressure, light, etc.), you can make just about anything interactive. There is even an accessory that lets the Arduino control a power cord for turning on house lights, for example. Sometime back I saw a project that used an RFID chip you carried in your pocket and, as you approached your car with your arms full of groceries, the Arduino would sense your presence (and *only* yours) and open the tailgate. Arduino applications span the spectrum from the whimsical to the serious. The choice is yours to make.

Does the Arduino make sense in schools? Of course it does. Aside from the obvious connection between this device and the practice of engineering, it provides a platform through which academic subjects from math to science can be explored with artifacts built by students themselves. For example, suppose students want to measure the speed of a marble rolling down an inclined plane for a series of inclinations. Using light sensors that change value as the marble passes in front of them, an Arduino board can be used to measure the time between marble detections. By using multiple sensors, acceleration can be measured as well, with the numerical results (time) being sent by the Arduino board to a computer screen in the form of a table.

Raspberry Pi

If the Arduino board is the interface between ideas and physical projects in the space of Life, then it is just possible that the Raspberry Pi (www.raspberrypi.org) and its offspring will become the interface between ideas and computer programs. Here the goal is the creation of an inexpensive computer tailor-made for students to create programs that can be shared with others in true constructionist fashion. This device, similar to the Arduino, ships as a circuit board with multiple connectors attached. But, instead of connections to lamps, motors, and sensors, it connects to keyboards and displays. In other words, it is a personal computer. What makes it interesting is that this device, fully assembled, costs only $35 (for the high-end model). It does not come with a power supply, a case, or even a keyboard and mouse. You are expected to provide all these things along with the display. The operating system for the Raspberry Pi is a version of Debian Linux—a robust environment that supports many great applications.

But the goal here is not just to have a cheap computer for running a word processor. It is to have a platform on which students can develop programs from scratch. If the Arduino takes us from ideas to physical objects, Raspberry Pi takes us from ideas to nonphysical programs that can be shared with others.

From the start, this was seen as a project driven by the needs of kids. The original idea came in 2006, when Eben Upton and his colleagues at the University of Cambridge's Computer Laboratory, Rob Mullins, Jack Lang, and Alan Mycroft, became concerned about the steady annual decline in the numbers and skills levels of the students applying to major in computer science. In the 1990s most of the kids applying were coming in as experienced hobbyist programmers, but this quickly changed and by the mid-2000s the Raspberry Pi team saw that something had been altered in the way kids were interacting with computers. Instead of learning to program, students were now using prebuilt software and thinking of web surfing as a meaningful computer experience. The idea they would craft programs of their own was, for many, a foreign concept.

In the early days of personal computing this was not the case. If you turned on an Apple II or a Commodore PET, you were greeted with a flashing cursor. What happened next was up to you. From this opening screen you could, if you wanted, write a program of your own. If you had some programs already saved on a tape cassette (or, later, a floppy disk), you could load and run these. But because there was so little commercial software available in the early days, most kids in school were taught to program—something that has all but disappeared, to our detriment.

WHAT'S NEXT?

I hope this chapter triggered some ideas about how you can use technology in powerful ways in the domain of Life to support what is being taught in the classroom. What would happen if we used technology to bring all four learning spaces into a single room? The next chapter highlights one such environment—the Educational Holodeck.

CHAPTER 11

Learning on the Holodeck

Imagine . . .

The crew is on a spaceship preparing for a six-month journey to Mars. The men and women on board represent many disciplines—geology, biology, engineering, vulcanology, medicine, and numerous others. The spaceship is quite large and has three decks, one devoted to human habitation; one for the growth of plants, chickens, and fish; and a third for power generation, waste recycling, and other tasks. The ship itself is a large toroid rotating at just the right speed to replicate the gravitational pull of Earth for everyone inside. The ship was built in space and never lands; it uses shuttle craft to go back and forth to planets.

Before the mission starts, the crew watches a short briefing video to learn the origin and importance of their mission. The goal of this mission is to explore whether Mars currently has life, or if it ever had life in the past. Thus far, remote observations are inconclusive on this topic, so it is time to send people there to check it out.

After completing the required checks of all systems on the spacecraft, the journey to Mars starts. But shortly after leaving Earth's orbit, sirens go off and the walls of the flight deck flash red, indicating there is a major problem. A quick look at the control computer screen shows that the outer shell of the spacecraft has been punctured by a piece of space debris and the ship is losing oxygen!

Fortunately, automatic doors have sealed off the area, which buys everyone a little time, but the next order of business is to solve this problem. A remote photo of the hole shows it to be a jagged mess, not a nicely formed circle. Everyone on the flight deck immediately goes to work designing a plug that can be built in the starship's replicator. Once built, this plug will be installed, and the mission can continue.

On arrival in orbit around Mars, the main viewport shows amazing details of the Red Planet—views simply not available from Earth. Because the goal is to search for life, the crew does research to see where people think evidence of current or prehistoric bacterial life forms might exist. As the ship orbits the planet, the striking features of Mars come into view—Olympus Mons, the largest mountain in our solar system; the huge canyon, Valles Marineris; and other features that make Mars so interesting to explore. The geologists and vulcanologists on board are fascinated, but the biologists are anxious to get started on their important task.

And then an emergency video from Earth shows up on a side screen. The NOAA spokesperson sends the following warning:

Attention all spacecraft in the inner solar system. This is the space weather prediction center on Earth. A radio blackout occurred yesterday when a M1 flare erupted on the sun. The huge coronal mass ejection, which includes many protons, is headed toward your location at about one million kilometers per hour. Check all radiation shields immediately! This storm presents a radiation danger to all life on your ship!

Having spent their life on Earth, protected from such disasters by the Van Allen belt, it occurs to some of the crew that Mars does not have this kind of automatic protection, and, if they stay where they are (on the sunny side of Mars), they will be getting direct hits from a storm. Their ship-based radiation shields are not prepared for a disaster of this magnitude.

The crew moves the ship to the dark side, letting Mars absorb the radiation and protecting the ship from any damage. After the storm passes, internal automatic damage reports show that this approach worked!

Finally, the crew has to decide if they want to send a team to the Martian surface, bring remotely collected samples back to the ship, or do all the collection and analysis remotely. Arguments quickly break out. The engineers want to use remote collection and sensing devices, and the biologists want to see the samples with their own eyes. The medical team argues that *if* Mars has active bacterial life, the chance of the ship having the proper antibiotics in case of infection is quite remote and everyone could die.

THE STORY BEHIND THE STORY

This scenario is not the plot of a science fiction movie, but is, instead, a description of a mission done by students in grades 4 through 6 on an Educational Holodeck—a simulation environment that can be used for myriad missions and adventures. To those taking part, the experience feels quite real.

ORIGIN OF THE EDUCATIONAL HOLODECK

In the years since first thinking about primordial learning spaces, I've shared my views on the topic and had the honor of seeing our work implemented in the design of schools. Personally, I have long wondered if a technology-enhanced environment could be built that incorporates all four learning spaces in such a fluid fashion that students could seamlessly move from space to space as they work on a specific project. Toward this end, I looked at lots of virtual spaces, including those found at the Disney parks and elsewhere. As a result of this protracted effort, I think I found a perfect space for students— the Educational Holodeck.

Gene Roddenberry's original "holodeck" has captured the imagination of millions since it first appeared in the TV series, *Star Trek: The Next Generation*. One 1993 episode, "Ship in a Bottle," takes place largely in this immersive virtual world where all objects are computer constructs, allowing the holodeck to become anything the users want—a Victorian living room, a pirate ship, and so on.[1]

One feature of this holodeck is that the virtual constructs are tangible. According to Roddenberry's vision, future haptic technology allows objects to be felt, picked up, even thrown around the room. Although haptic holography is in its infancy today, many of the features and benefits of the holodeck can be built with inexpensive existing technology, and can be used to provide rich immersive educational experiences for learners of any age.

Years ago, MIT professor Janet Murray predicted in her book, *Hamlet on the Holodeck,* that the nature of narrative would change as a result of the growth of interactive software and the web.[2] More recent work at Google has resulted in the Liquid Galaxy (www.google.com/earth/explore/showcase/liquidgalaxy.html), an immersive virtual "elevator" with which a participant can navigate the entire planet using a special version of Google Earth. The downside of Liquid Galaxy is that it is currently restricted to a few people at a time, not a classroom full of students. That said, the resulting environment is staggering. Users feel more like they are on a ride than using a piece of software. The fact that users are already familiar with the software does not diminish the willingness to suspend disbelief—a feature of well-designed immersive environments in general.

Similarly immersive environments are the staple of the Disney parks, whether it is taking a trip into space or hang-gliding over the California landscape. These short but powerful experiences are so popular there are usually long lines of people waiting to get on the "rides." I say "rides" because, although you may feel you are on a ride, you are actually not going very far—a few feet or less.

In this book we define an Educational Holodeck as a reconfigurable immersive learning space in which tasks are carried out in support of various "missions," each of which has strong curricular ties. Each mission is formulated in the context of a systemic operation that is transdisciplinary to the extent it cuts across subject areas and supports learner inquiry and in-depth projects. This physical environment stands in stark contrast to traditional classrooms. Educational Holodecks embrace all four learning spaces: Campfires, Watering Holes, Caves, and Life. During a mission, students migrate seamlessly thorough these spaces as they do their work. There is no specific Cave time, for example. If a student needs to try something out in a reflective environment, the Educational Holodeck supports that, even while other students may be availing themselves of information gleaned from the other three spaces. Our work in this area resulted in a short documentary done through George Lucas's *Edutopia* project.[3]

Some educators have recognized the shortcomings of a traditional classroom and turned their rooms into interactive domains where students can, for example, role-play grand historical events. This type of teaching was a subplot in the 1984 film *Teachers*, in which a mental outpatient (played by Richard Mulligan) accepts a job as a substitute history teacher in a beleaguered school, and is loved by the students because he has them enact historical events such as Washington crossing the Delaware.[4] His adventures took place in an otherwise usual classroom that was transformed through costumes and props. Many teachers have recognized the value of having students reenact historical events. For one thing, they are far more likely to remember what they have learned. Another result of this kind of learning is that students are eager to participate, and even express disappointment when the school day ends. Rather than see history (for example) as a boring list of names, dates, and battles, it is seen as a vibrant study of the past from which we learn a great deal about today and the future. The same can be said for virtually any other discipline.

Today we have the opportunity to build extremely engaging learning environments that bridge the gap between the 1984 vision and the holodeck of the future. In our Educational Holodeck, role-playing is moved to a very high level.

EPISTEMIC GAMES AND EPISTEMIC FRAMES

Right now you might be thinking, "Great—just what we need—another game for kids to play instead of spending their time learning useful things." The Educational Holodeck envisioned here is not a video game but it is a game of sorts—a very special kind of game. Professor David Shaffer points out that games are activities that have rules and roles—a definition that cuts a wide swath.[5] And within that swath lie what he calls *epistemic games,* games that simulate systems in ways that help people develop their frame for thinking about the subject. He calls this the *epistemic frame* and it has five components:

- Skills
- Knowledge
- Identity
- Values
- Epistemology

The first two of these are the traditional content of schooling. When we teach physics, we expect students to learn some of the skills and knowledge associated with that discipline. But a student could go through an entire course without once having any idea how physicists view themselves (their identity), what values they hold, or how they think. (And by this last point we don't mean the "scientific method.") If a student is exposed only to the content of a discipline, how can we expect anyone to develop a passion in the subject that might lead to a lifelong career? Every subject has its own epistemic frame—and each one is different.

I have multiple frames as part of my system. My frame as a grandfather is different from my frame as an educator or as an engineer or mathematician. The more passionate one is about a field, the stronger the frame becomes. This was brought home to me years ago when I was scheduled to speak at the International Space Development

Conference. I called a friend at NASA and asked if she would be attending. Her response was priceless; "Oh, no, David. That is a conference for engineers and I'm a scientist." That observation hit me like a ton of bricks. Her identity was quite clear! (As for the conference, after my speech I got to hang out with Rusty Schweickart and some other pioneering astronauts, so I had a ball!)

For this reason, we designed the Educational Holodeck to be an epistemic game, and students do far more than acquire skills and knowledge—they also start to develop and understand identity, values, and thinking methods (epistemology) of the roles they are playing. This is achieved through role-playing. For the duration of a mission, students adopt roles of the kinds of crew members that would be needed if the mission were real—geologists, medical doctors, biologists, and so on. By immersing themselves in the activity through their particular lens they are able to learn something about the identity, values, and thinking methods employed by practitioners in the field they have chosen.

ADDITIONAL VALUES OF EDUCATIONAL HOLODECKS

We've made the point in this book that technology use in education to date largely replicates learning models of the past. Instead of physical libraries, many students do research on the Internet. Instead of reading paper books, some schools are looking at e-book readers. Yes, powerful computers are still being used to provide directed instruction and to measure competence using multiple-choice examinations, but the true power of modern technologies lies hidden. Nowhere is this more evident than in the use of technology in support of the lecture-based classroom. As we've said earlier, in this kind of environment, the move to a more inquiry-centric, project-based approach to education is very difficult.

Our goal was to create a learning environment for which the traditional lecture-based model *cannot* be sustained—an environment in which students are freed to explore domains of understanding and knowledge through direct experiences. Imagine, for example, the difference between a teacher showing a NASA image of Saturn on a screen and giving a lecture on the rings versus students being able to be on the bridge of a starship where they can fly to a computer model of Saturn themselves, explore the rings in detail, and use a variety of resources to help them understand more of what they are seeing. If the software provides the latest NASA images of Saturn, they may well believe that are close to the planet as it fills the main viewport.

We think of the Educational Holodeck as a theater without audiences in that everyone in the room is part of a mission. There is no place for lectures here because there is no audience—only participants.

The kinds of topics students can explore on the holodeck is limited only by their imagination, the teacher's willingness to be a co-learner and fellow explorer on the activity, and the support resources needed to sustain the simulation. Potential topics include the following:

- Space exploration
- Exploring the oceans
- The geology of the earth
- Geography
- Atmosphere and weather
- Navigating through the human body
- Exploring atoms and molecules
- Traveling through time to historical events
- Exploring the challenge (and desirability) of communicating with distant civilizations in which students explore the role of myth in our own culture and ask if we can truly communicate with a distant civilization without understanding their core stories and beliefs (This mission is described in the following.)

Essential to all these domains are the crosscurricular connections that can be made. Students can acquire the skills taught in traditional classes through their engagement as active participants in this new world.

One example is a mission currently in design that lasts an entire semester, only part of the time in the Educational Holodeck itself. The mission is based on NASA research showing the possible presence of "Goldilocks" planets in the region being explored by the Kepler Space Telescope.[6] These planets are not too hot, not too cold, not too big, and not too small—in other words they are just the right size to support life. (In *Star Trek* terms, these are called class M planets—a designation used privately by some NASA scientists, but not used by them in public.)

The proposed mission for our project is the following: having identified possible planets that can support intelligent life, we will visit them to see what exists. On the way we intercept a coded message coming from the target planet. The first task is for the students to break the code. Once this is done they need to decide if they want to respond, thus letting the planet know we are in the area.

This, alone, is a nontrivial exercise but then it gets even better. As the journey proceeds, other questions arise. Whatever language the natives of this planet are using, it is not likely to be similar to any languages on Earth, or is it? And, let's say we do understand the words of the language, will we be able to communicate effectively without both sides knowing the myths and legends that shape our use of language in deep ways? For example, on our own planet, where multiple languages are the norm, is there a core of myths and stories that cut across cultures? What role do these stories have on our views of ourselves, and how often do we use them in sharing ideas with others—even if we use them unconsciously? Some of the major ideas of this mission were explored in a graduate course I taught many years ago entitled *Metaphor, Myth, and Multimedia* in which students ended up crafting their own life-based stories as a multimedia project. But the topic is not just for graduate students. Middle and high school students could explore the topic just as well!

So far this mission explores topics in mathematics, language, linguistics, cultural history, and folklore—and that is just for starters. Instead of watching a science fiction TV series, students will define and design the core elements of their mission, doing the kinds of things professionals in the field will do when such missions become possible.

WHY IT MATTERS

From a pedagogical perspective, the Educational Holodeck facilitates the movement of students to the boundary between anxiety and flow (using the terminology of Csikszentmihalyi). As mentioned previously, this construct reveals a major problem with lecture-based delivery—the diversity of skill levels in any classroom makes it impossible to meet the needs of all learners simultaneously through teacher-directed lectures. Csikszentmihalyi's research has shown that the anxiety-flow boundary of the challenge-skill diagram is home to optimal learning experiences and is a place people will put themselves when they have the chance.

People want to be close to flow whenever they can and to approach it from the anxiety side. This characteristic of the boundary between anxiety and flow accounts for the popularity of many video games. They create some anxiety but not so much as to shut down the willingness to play. Once players enter the flow region, the game level increases putting them on the brink of anxiety yet again.

There are five key elements of Educational Holodeck learning that lead to engagement:

- Immersive
- Interactive
- Interesting
- Interdisciplinary
- Innovative

These five elements all lead to engagement, meaning that the Educational Holodeck experience will be remembered for a long time. Remember the Mars mission at the start of this chapter? A year or so later, we brought several of the students in to see what they remembered. Some had continued their studies of Mars on their own, and one child wanted to know what it would take for him to become an astronaut! We also did some exploration of what students knew about Mars before the mission and what they had learned. The results were quite heartening. For example, before the mission some students thought the following about Mars:

- It is hot.
- It is red.
- It is a solid planet.
- It is close to the asteroid belt.
- You can see it with your eyes.
- It does not have life.

Some of these are true, and some are not. When the question was posed after the mission, the results were more accurate and greater in number—just what we would expect if students had actually learned anything. For example, after the mission, students reported the following things about Mars:

- It might have life in the interior.
- It has ice.
- It is cold.
- Humans never went there before.
- It has two moons, Deimos and Phobos.
- It has methane gas plumes in the spring.
- There was probably lots of water there in the past.
- It might have bacteria.
- It has the largest mountain in the solar system.

- Space travelers can get osteoporosis and atrial fibrillation.
- It has less gravitational pull than Earth.
- Mar receives lots of cosmic radiation.

Some of these observations were expected and others (medical problems associated with space travel) were not. It is important to remember that, except for a five-minute video setting forth the goal of the mission, there was no lecture nor was there any list of required reading materials. The students did all the work on their own. The job of the adults in the room was to facilitate the process.

BUILDING AN EDUCATIONAL HOLODECK

Because holographic displays are in their infancy, a model for our Educational Holodecks makes use of relatively inexpensive existing technology. The first (and hardest) challenge is finding a location for the deck. A simple effective configuration can be built in an existing classroom, provided that the furniture is movable and the projection and computer technology is available. Ideally, it would be an otherwise unused room. The room would be windowless and rectangular. If the room has windows, these can be covered with boards sealed flush with the walls. The entire room would be painted white and used only for Educational Holodeck events. Because there is no visual connection to the world outside, participants can easily get the feeling that what they are experiencing is "real." Our first Educational Holodeck could accommodate twenty students or more at a time—a good-sized group for our projects.

The next step is to provide the capacity to cover each of the walls with images showing the interior surfaces of, for example, a starship. This can be done with special slide projectors using images that define the wall patterns and so on. Because these images do not change during a single simulation, there is no need to spend money on video projectors for background images. Alternatively, wall coloring during a mission can be provided by computer-controlled lights, which alone are quite effective (and inexpensive).

"Viewports" will require either computer projectors or large flat-screen monitors. For example, a starship's bridge might have a viewport into space at the front, with data screens on one or both sides. Other props (flashing lights, etc.) can be provided as needed. The interior design of the Educational Holodeck could even be an art project done by the students themselves. For the Mars mission we used HyperStudio to build the ship's control panel. When certain buttons were pressed on the interactive whiteboard on which the HyperStudio-based control panel was projected, scripts were sent to the Celestia software whose images were projected on a screen 10 meters wide and 1.5 meters high. This screen was our viewport into space. Because HyperStudio can also send messages to the Arduino board, it is easy to have the color of the walls change to red, for example, in case of an emergency on board the craft.

The interior of the room can be outfitted with furniture providing seating and equipment for the crew (see figure 11.1). Each crew member is a member of a team and has specific tasks and a computer terminal and other tools from which these tasks can be carried out. The captain (who may or may not be the teacher) would direct the adventure from a special seat. The room should also have a good sound system (with subwoofers) so that when alarms go off they are dramatic, or, for example, if an Educational Holodeck submarine hits the ocean floor, this should be accompanied by a loud scraping sound. Multiple computers make it easy for many things to be happening at once (just as in the real world). This fits with today's students' comfort with multitasking and builds creative tension into the activity. One of the key elements is to avoid having cables on the floor where they can be tripped over. This makes tablets useful tools for students when they are doing web-based research, but access to full computers is still required for other tasks. In this case, computers are placed along walls and computer controls that are not done with the interactive whiteboard can be done with wireless keyboards and mice.

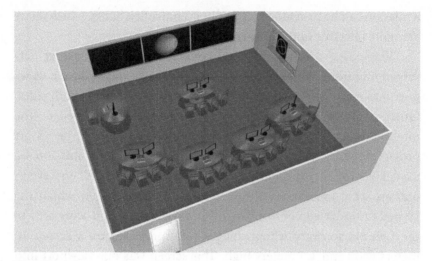

Figure 11.1

In addition to computer systems, microscopes and other tools can be incorporated in special areas in the room. For example, a sample of red clay could be teleported from the Martian surface for microscopic analysis by students who, with a digital microscope, could display their images on a viewport for everyone to see.

Assuming much of the computing equipment already exists in the school, it is possible that a fully equipped Educational Holodeck could be built for $10,000 to $20,000—maybe much less than that. For example, many schools have enough computers to run the simulations. The viewport requires either multiple projectors or side-by-side large displays to show the view out the front of the simulation. Other expenses include a 3D fabricator (for missions in which parts need to be made to repair damages to the ship), and the price of these is under $2,000. This system can also be used in other classrooms when the Educational Holodeck is not being used. Assuming the only purchases are three ceiling-mounted projectors (projected onto a smooth wall painted with flat white paint), a multiple display controller for the main computer, and the 3D fabricator, the cost is likely to be just under $10,000, and is dropping every year.

The critical component is not the mechanical aspects of the room but the deep pedagogical shift educators will make when using this environment. This pedagogical shift can be facilitated through an understanding of the Knights of Knowledge materials described in chapter 7.

HOLODECK SOFTWARE

Effective software is one of the keys to making a functional Educational Holodeck. Students can help find the software tools themselves. For example, for space exploration, the free Celestia program (www.shatters.net/celestia) is amazingly good for the front viewport. Images for the other screens are brought into view by teams showing what they have found to help the mission achieve its goal. This means that any student computer or tablet must be able to have its image directed to a wall-based screen in the room. Although students will find these resources on their own, rich libraries of space-related images (for example) can be found at NASA's website (www.nasa.gov).

Aside from the crew actually driving the craft, other student teams will be needed to conduct research on the items being explored. This can be done using the Internet on their own computers and other tools for gathering and analyzing data. Although much of this research would be done during the mission, before using the Educational Holodeck students would need to prepare for their voyage and fully understand their roles in the adventure. This preparation would take place in the days preceding their first use of the system.

CREATION OF MISSIONS

Even if you never build an Educational Holodeck for your school, the process we use for developing missions is relevant to the building of any project-based learning task.

The first step is to define the mission. This is the most critical part. Although you may want to develop something related to a curricular topic, transdisciplinarity is the key—so avoid defining the challenge in narrow terms. As for overall mission length, this will often be dictated by the topic—missions that cut across many disciplines will likely last longer than those that just focus primarily on one area. This said, we've found that the time spent in the Educational Holodeck itself should be at least two hours at a stretch. This allows for the willing suspension of disbelief to the point that students think they are actually on (for example) a spaceship. The students will think they have only been there for a few minutes, and it is common for them to complain when you let them know they are done for the day. In our case, this meant doing missions during after-school periods.

When it comes to mission design, a good starting point is the formulation of a driving question—one for which it is possible that no one knows the answer. Aside from the critical element of putting kids on a real adventure, it also makes the missions "Google-proof."

Risk is essential—all missions have things happen that are unexpected and students need to learn how to respond creatively in these situations. These risks have high-stakes consequences (e.g., the crew dies if the challenge is not met). This not only focuses the students' attention, but it also keeps the level of excitement high.

Next, the mission designer should create a short didactic presentation video to set the stage for the mission. The Knights of Knowledge framework we described in chapter 7 is perfect, although the video might be longer than a minute in length. Our Mars mission, for example, starts with a five-minute video that describes why people have thought life exists on Mars for a long time, highlights current NASA research on the topic, and then sets the stage for the current mission.

Any mission is likely to take advantage of many technological tools ranging from software to specialized devices such as 3D fabricators or CNC machines. The software that runs during the mission then needs to be written. In our work, we use HyperStudio for this task. Not only can HyperStudio run scripts for other software (such as Celestia, for example), but it can also send signals to the Arduino controller to run room lights and other devices in the room that should be under computer control. This control software for the mission should be visible on a touch screen where switches can be pressed by students to control the mission.

This is a big task, one that requires commitment and dedication, but the responses from the students are worth the effort. And a single mission can be used with a wide variety of grade levels. The only difference will be in the sophistication of the work done by the kids. To be honest, younger students (e.g., fourth grade) often come up with the most creative ideas. All too often we put kids in predefined boxes defining their abilities, but they often surprise us when given a real challenge to address.

HOW TO USE THE EDUCATIONAL HOLODECK

Because the Educational Holodeck is immersive and dynamic, multitasking is commonplace; this is not an environment conducive to lectures. It is, as I said previously, a stage on which there is no audience, only actors. Everyone will have a role to play to ensure the success of the mission. The learning opportunities for such an environment are incredible.

Once built, the Educational Holodeck may find its first uses in science courses in which students visit remote sites, explore, and learn about what they find there. Prior to starting their mission, the students need to define their own roles and responsibilities as crew members—who will be piloting the craft? Who will be doing research on the scientific portion of the mission? Who will attend to the technology itself?

Next, students need to explore other questions: why are we embarking on this mission? What resources will we need? How long will the mission take? What questions do we hope to answer as a result of our trip? Myriad other questions can be developed, all of which become impetus for research prior to and after completion of the mission itself. Through these questions, the content of the mission is clarified, and students will locate and learn this content themselves with the teacher's help.

If students are allowed to choose their destination for each journey, they can build a body of knowledge that, through this intensely immersive experience, will likely stay with them forever. If the traditional classroom was based on extrinsic motivation, the Educational Holodeck is home to intrinsic motivation and, potentially, a new way of teaching and learning that can engage all learners.

OUR FIRST EDUCATIONAL HOLODECK

Our first installation was done in a school in Recife, Brazil. We were given a room and the support needed to build out the system. My plan was to have the Educational Holodeck functional by November of that year. In late September I received a call from someone in the Federal Ministry of Education asking if we would be ready in time for World Space Week. This annual event (from October 4 to 10) was declared by the General Assembly of the United Nations to celebrate each year at the international level the contributions of space science and technology to the betterment of the human condition.

I said, "Sure." Boy, were the following days busy! We got the project running well enough to conduct our Mars mission. Our entry was one of only five from Brazil that year—and it was the only one located in a school. Of course, none of this mattered to the kids. They were signing themselves up for the trip of a lifetime (see figure 11.2)!

The images in figures 11.3 and 11.4 show students working on the Educational Holodeck during the mission to Mars.

Figure 11.2

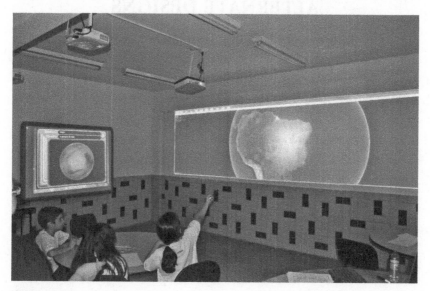

Figure 11.3

Figure 11.4

ALTERNATE DESIGNS

We aren't the only ones thinking about interactive, immersive learning environments. For example, Wooranna Park Primary School (www.woorannaparkps.vic.edu.au) is an amazing school in a suburb of Melbourne, Australia. The overall design of the school incorporates many kinds of learning spaces, including what Principal Ray Trotter calls *stimulating learning platforms* (SLPs). These are physical spaces (a model of a boat, for example) on which students can navigate to different locations and take part in crossdisciplinary adventures. The boat capitalizes on children's imagination to make voyages using Google Sea, for example. These imaginary voyages place children in lifelike situations in which they are forced to grapple with complicated mathematical and scientific principles. How far is it to New Zealand? What direction do I turn the boat's compass to? How fast are we traveling? How long will it take to get there? The children are also learning Morse code and communicating via naval flags.

Figure 11.5
Source: Courtesy of Raymond Trotter.

The SLPs have allowed teachers to tap into children's imagination to create learning environments that, despite their imaginary nature, are very authentic to them as well as being highly experiential and interdisciplinary. These environments are often launching pads to further experiences. They also give credence to the importance of children's creative play in supporting their learning.

From my perspective, these environments meet the criteria of Educational Holodecks, although they are not as immersive as ours. For example, they have created their own version of a starship from which students can go on multiple missions to planets and the far reaches of the universe (see figure 11.5).

Other SLPs at Wooranna include one designed for time travel—useful for exploring everything from history to dinosaurs. Over time I expect to see more of these kinds of environments in schools as we continue to shift our focus in the direction of project-based learning.

One feature of the SLPs created in Australia is that they are very inexpensive to create, as long as the learning space is open and flexible.

FROM THE CAMPFIRE TO THE HOLODECK

In chapter 1 I presented the idea that learning should be an adventure, not a dreaded chore. As we look at too many schools today, they seem primarily focused on Campfire learning—the directed-instruction model in which students are told what they "need" to know, with precious little time left to explore the other learning environments through which true understanding develops.

My goal was to show a path from the Campfire to the holodeck—a path filled with boundless opportunities for exploration and discovery, some of which can be applied in every classroom immediately, whereas others require some investment of time and money to make real. I surely do not expect you to rush out and install an Educational Holodeck at your school, but there are many other things you can do to make the adventure of learning joyous for all—yourself included.

If some of the ideas presented here have sparked some excitement and opportunity for you, I will have succeeded.

Notes

Introduction

1. D. D. Thornburg, *Campfires in Cyberspace* (Starsong Publications, 1999).
2. P. Nair and R. Fielding, *The Language of School Design: Design Patterns for 21st Century Schools,* Fully Revised 2nd Edition (Designshare, 2009).

Chapter 1: The Problem with Traditional Classrooms

1. H. Rugg and A. Shumaker, *The Child-Centered School: An Appraisal of the New Education* (Yonkers, NY: World Book Company, 1928), 302–303.
2. N.V.N. Chism and D. J. Bickford, eds., *New Directions for Teaching and Learning: The Importance of Physical Space in Creating Supportive Learning Environments* (San Francisco: Jossey-Bass, 2003).
3. R. Gerver, *Creating Tomorrow's Schools Today: Education—Our Children—Their Futures* (Stafford, UK: Network Educational Press, 2010).
4. M. Csikszentmihalyi, *Flow: The Psychology of Optimal Experience* (New York: Harper Perennial Modern Classics, 2008).
5. M. Csikszentmihalyi, K. Rathunde, and S. Whalen, *Talented Teenagers: The Roots of Success and Failure* (Cambridge, UK: Cambridge University Press, 1996).
6. W. H. Kilpatrick, "W. H. The 'Project Method': Child-Centeredness in Progressive Education," *Teachers College Record* 19 (1918): 319–334.

Chapter 2: Campfires

1. G. McDermott, *Raven: A Trickster Tale from the Pacific Northwest* (San Anselmo, CA: Sandpiper, 2001).

Chapter 3: Watering Holes

1. Revista TAM, "Um Novo Jeito de Conversar" [A New Way of Conversing], *Nas Nuvens* (2012). Available online at www.tamnasnuvens.com .br/revista/site/zoom.html?path=content/image/2012/abril/popup /&id=61&qtd=164.
2. L. Vygotsky, *Mind and Society: The Development of Higher Psychological Processes* (Cambridge, MA: Harvard University Press, 1978).
3. M. Mastrangeli, M. Schmidt, and L. Lacasa, "The Roundtable: An Abstract Model of Conversation Dynamics," *Journal of Artificial Societies and Social Simulation* 13, no. 2 (2010).
4. United Nations Educational, Scientific and Cultural Organization (UNESCO), *Working Paper Series on Mobile Learning.* Available online at www.unesco.org/new/en/unesco/themes/icts/m4ed/mobile-learning -resources/unescomobilelearningseries.

Chapter 4: Caves

1. B. J. Wadsworth, *Piaget's Theory of Cognitive and Affective Development: Foundations of Constructivism* (Boston: Allyn & Bacon, 2003).
2. Edna St. Vincent Millay, excerpt from "Upon this age, that never speaks its mind" from *Collected Poems.* Copyright 1939, © 1967 by Edna St. Vincent Millay and Normal Millay Ellis. Reprinted with the permission of The Permissions Company, Inc., on behalf of Holly Peppe, Literary Executor, The Millay Society. www.millay.org.
3. W. Stukeley, *Memoirs of Sir Isaac Newton's Life* (London: Taylor and Francis, 1936 [1752]).
4. D. D. Thornburg, United States Patent 4121153—Tapered resistor meter (1978).

Chapter 5: Life

1. I. Harel and S. Papert, *Constructionism* (Norwood, NJ: Ablex Publishing, 1991).
2. G. Tulley and J. Spiegler, *50 Dangerous Things* (New York: NAL Trade, 2011).

3. G. Tulley, *Tinkering School.* Available online at www.tinkeringschool.com.
4. G. Tulley, *The Brightworks Arc.* Available online at http://sfbrightworks .org/the-brightworks-arc.
5. *The Makerspace Playbook* (2012). Available online at http://makerspace .com/wp-content/uploads/2012/04/makerspaceplaybook-201204.pdf.

Chapter 6: The Challenge of Technology

1. J. Ohler, *Storytelling and New Media Narrative.* Available online at www .jasonohler.com/storytelling/storyeducation.cfm.
2. M. McLuhan and E. McLuhan, *Laws of Media: The New Science* (Toronto: University of Toronto Press, 1992).
3. *Popular Mechanics* (1949).
4. T. Malone and L. Black, "Cell Phones Step Up in Class," *Chicago Tribune* (October 12, 2010): 1.
5. F. Prose, "Why Are Poor Kids Paying for School Security?" *New York Review of Books* (December 12, 2012). Available online at www.nybooks .com/blogs/nyrblog/2012/dec/12/poor-kids-paying-school-security.
6. Amanda Lenhart, *Teens, Smartphones and Texting.* Pew Research Center's Internet and American Life Project (March 19, 2012). Available online at www.pewinternet.org/~/media//Files/Reports/2012/PIP _Teens_Smartphones_and_Texting.pdf.
7. Eric Zeman, "Why Android's Dominance Is Bad," *InformationWeek-Hardware.* Available online at www.informationweek.com/hardware /handheld/why-androids-dominance-is-bad/240142134.
8. D. Hewitt, F. W. Friendly, and S. Steinberg, *The Edward R. Murrow Collection* (CBS Television, 2005).
9. M. Loukides, "App Inventor and the Culture Wars," *O'Reilly Radar* (July 15, 2010). Available online at http://radar.oreilly.com/2010/07 /culture-wars.html.

Chapter 7: Technological Campfires

1. Slashdot, *Open Textbooks Win over Publishers in CA* (August 13, 2009). Available online at http://news.slashdot.org/story/09/08/13/1450220 /open-textbooks-win-over-publishers-in-ca.

2. "Johnny Lee Demos Wii Remote Hacks," *TED.com* (April 2008). Available online at www.ted.com/talks/johnny_lee_demos_wii_remote_hacks.html.
3. Buck Institute for Education, *What Is PBL?* Available online at www.bie.org/about/what_is_pbl.

Chapter 8: Technological Watering Holes

1. C. Wood, E. Jackson, L. Hart, B. Plester, and L. Wilde, "The Effect of Text Messaging on 9- and 10-year-old Children's Reading, Spelling and Phonological Processing Skills," *Journal of Computer Assisted Learning* 27 (2011): 28–36.
2. Pew Internet and American Life Project, *Photos and Videos as Social Currency.* Available online at www.pewinternet.org/~/media//Files/Reports/2012/PIP_OnlineLifeinPictures_PDF.pdf.
3. Erick Schonfeld, "Netflix Now the Largest Single Source of Internet Traffic in North America," *TechCrunch* (May 17, 2011). Available online at http://techcrunch.com/2011/05/17/netflix-largest-internet-traffic.
4. Cecelia Kang, "Verizon Wireless to Offer Free Voice and Texting, Boost Cost for Data Use," *Washington Post* (June 12, 2012). Available online at http://articles.washingtonpost.com/2012-06-12/business/35461021_1_2-gigabyte-plan-verizon-wireless-expensive-plans.
5. S. Winchester, *The Professor and the Madman: A Tale of Murder, Insanity, and the Making of the* Oxford English Dictionary (New York: Harper Perennial, 2005).
6. *Wikipedia:Rules* (2012). Available online at http://simple.wikipedia.org/w/index.php?title=Wikipedia:Rules&oldid=3949048.
7. *The Peerogogy Handbook.* Available online at http://peeragogy.org.
8. Paulo Blikstein, *Travels in Troy with Freire.* Available online at www.blikstein.com/paulo/documents/books/Blikstein-TravelsInTroyWithFreire.pdf.
9. S. Higgins, E. Mercier, L. Burd, and A. Joyce-Gibbons, "Multi-touch Tables and Collaborative Learning," *British Journal of Educational Technology* 43 (2012): 1041–1054.

Chapter 9: Technological Caves

1. Seymour Papert. Available online at http://web.media.mit.edu/~papert.
2. "Logo (Programming Language)," *Wikipedia* (2012). Available online at http://en.wikipedia.org/w/index.php?title=Logo_(programming _language)&oldid=527646190.
3. Seymour Papert, "Hard Fun." Available online at www.papert.org/articles /HardFun.html.

Chapter 10: Technological Life Spaces

1. *A Private Universe*. Available online at www.learner.org/resources /series28.html?pop=yes&pid=9#.
2. C. Anderson, *Makers: The New Industrial Revolution* (New York: Crown Business, 2012).

Chapter 11: Learning on the Holodeck

1. "Ship in a Bottle (*Star Trek: The Next Generation*)," *Wikipedia* (2012). Available online at http://en.wikipedia.org/w/index.php?title=Ship_in _a_Bottle_(Star_Trek:_The_Next_Generation)&oldid=521224929.
2. J. H. Murray, *Hamlet on the Holodeck: The Future of Narrative in Cyberspace* (Cambridge, MA: MIT Press, 1998).
3. "David Thornburg on the Evolving Classroom (Big Thinkers Series)," *Edutopia*. Available online at www.edutopia.org/david-thornburg -future-classroom-video.
4. A. Hiller, *Teachers* (MGM, 2007).
5. D. W. Shaffer, *How Computer Games Help Children Learn* (London: Palgrave Macmillan, 2008).
6. D. Koch et al., "Kepler: A Space Mission to Detect Earth-Class Exoplanets," *Space Telescopes and Instruments V*, SPIE Conference Proceedings (1998).

Index

Page references followed by *fig* indicate an illustrated figure.